BY

RICHARD LIVINGSTONE

EDITED AND INTRODUCED BY

J. E. B. MUNSON, M.A., D.Phil.

TABB HOUSE

This edition first published 1988 TABB HOUSE,
11 Church Street, Padstow, Cornwall, PL28 8BG

Published in association with the Farmington Institute
for Christian Studies - Oxford

First published by Cambridge University Press, 1943.

ISBN 0 907018 43 2

Typeset by St George Typesetting, Redruth, Cornwall
Printed in Great Britain by A. Wheaton & Co. Ltd., Exeter

CONTENTS

EDITOR'S INTRODUCTION

THE YEAR 1942 was one of the most decisive in the Second World War. By its end it seemed that at last the tide was turning in the Allies' favour. The German attempt to break out of Stalingrad had failed and in North Africa British and American troops had launched their Desert Campaign against Italian and German forces. Although Singapore had fallen to the horrors of Japanese occupation, American forces had counter-attacked in the Coral Sea, at Midway and Guadalcanal. At last light was beginning to appear at the end of the tunnel.

At home, the war had seen a tremendous outpouring of discussion and debate about the sort of society men wanted to see when victory and peace came. If man could destroy so much of his world through war, could he not rebuild a better one when the destruction had ended? The war effort seemed to raise life to a new and higher level, as King George VI had noted in his 1941 Christmas message to the Empire: 'It is in serving each other and in sacrificing for our common good that we are finding our true life. In that spirit we shall win the War, and in that same spirit we shall win for the world after the War a true and lasting peace.'

Far away from the war, but not from the discussions, in the quiet of Corpus Christi College, Oxford, the college president, Sir Richard Livingstone, sat down to reflect. For many years Sir Richard had been known not just as a highly skilled classicist but as an earnest advocate both of reform in university and schools and of extending educational opportunities for women. Securing an education worthy of those efforts which the war had called forth was one of the most important topics being discussed, as the King had noted:

> I would say to the coming generation, the boys and girls of today, the men and women of tomorrow, train yourself in body, mind and spirit so as to be ready for whatever part you may be called to play and for the tasks which will await you as citizens of the Empire when the War is over. We must all, older and younger, resolve that having been entrusted with so great a cause, that at whatever cost, God

helping us, we will not falter or fail.*

The training in 'body, mind and spirit' raised another question — the quality of that training which all agreed should be more widely available. Sir Richard therefore, throughout 1942, pondered the nature of the education which a victorious country should seek. He was not alone for not too far away, in the New Building at Magdalen College, another scholar, C. S. Lewis, pondered the same question. The British achievements in literature and constitutional government, her heritage as a Christian society based on law which protected and enhanced the subject's freedom, and her legacy of a free economy underlying and securing all these: none of this rich heritage was self-renewing. It needed to be passed on, undiluted as Lewis wrote in *The Abolition of Man*:

> The task of the modern educator is not to cut down jungles but to irrigate deserts. The right defence against false sentiments is to inculcate just sentiments. By starving the sensibility of our pupils we only make them easier prey to the propagandist when he comes. For famished nature will be avenged and a hard heart is no infallible protection against a soft head.†

Scholars like Livingstone and Lewis knew that there were forces about which would not only refuse to hand on what had been given them in trust but actually to deny to children the heritage that their fathers were fighting to retain: worst of all, these people would deny it in the very name of education itself. These so-called reformers would create that desert to which Lewis had referred. As Livingstone wrote in *Education for a World Adrift*, 'The vocational and the social aspects of education are essential, but' he went on, 'the most fatal to omit is the spiritual aspect; fatal, because its absence may be long unperceived, and, as with an insidious disease, a State may suffer from it and be unconscious of its condition till the complaint has gone too far to cure.'

The 'spiritual aspect' to Livingstone was not just the passing on of the British heritage of Christian faith but the very quality of education and through it, of life itself. No generation lives in a vacuum: the land on which we live has been lived on by our ancestors who lie under its soil; the problems we face are more often than not versions of the problems they faced and the range of moral choices open to us was open to them. History did not lead up to our generation and stop; rather, we are just one more stage in these islands' long and rich history.

To Sir Richard Livingstone these 'reformers' would erase our national memory and deny children a knowledge of that context — racial, religious and historical — in which they lived. He did not know, of course, how serious the problem would grow. Some readers will be surprised to know that in the 1930s there were those who wished to remove or at least diminish Christian teaching in our state schools. Others will be surprised to know that the levelling tendencies of mass democracy were so evident at the same time: to men like Livingstone great men stood like markers to remind us of our past, of our successes and our failures as Britons, as Christians and as civilised Europeans. Socrates, Sir Thomas More, St Bernard, Lord Shaftesbury, Plato, Dante, Shakespeare, Wordsworth: these are the men — not Mr Nelson Mandela or Mr Che Guevara — whom 'all ages and universal assent would regard. . .as masters in the art of living'.*

Richard Winn Livingstone was born on 23 January 1880. His father was the Reverend Richard John Livingstone, product of a clerical family and Vicar of Aigburth, Liverpool. His mother was the Hon. Millicent Allanson Winn, daughter of the third Baron Headley, an Irish peer: Livingstone was always proud of his Irish blood. His father was eventually made an honorary Canon of Liverpool Cathedral but died when Livingstone was twenty-seven. The young boy was sent to Winchester and proceeded to New College, Oxford where he was Hertford Scholar. He read Classics and did extremely well, earning a double first in Honour Moderations and then in Literae Humaniores. He also won a variety of University prizes including the Chancellor's Latin Prize (which was published by the Oxford bookseller, B. H. Blackwell) and the Thomas Arnold Historical Essay Prize.

It surprised no one that he stayed on in Oxford to become a Classics don although some at New College were surprised (and one suspects annoyed) that he 'migrated' to Corpus Christi College to become tutor and Fellow although Corpus had a high reputation for classical scholarship. Although friends commented on his 'somewhat dreamy manner' they recognised tht underneath the exterior the young don had a 'certainty of purpose'. He was, as *The Times* said at his death, 'the humanist *par excellence*' for 'in him the Greek and the Christian inheritance formed a blend so perfect that it was difficult for him to realise how others found contradictions in its composing elements'.

Livingstone was no cloistered scholar, remote from the world about him: far from it. The first decade of the twentieth century was a time of fierce debate about education, both in Parliament and in the country at large and the debate continued until the very eve of war in 1914. Livingstone became one of the young dons then campaigning for a wide-ranging reform at Oxford from within. The battles, as befits academics, were fought out in the columns of *The Times* and the Liberal daily, the *Westminster Gazette*. The subject was also raised in the House of Lords by Bishop Gore of Birmingham, himself something of a High Church *enfant terrible*. Livingstone's great ally was the Reverend William Temple, a Fellow of Queen's College and a son of Frederick Temple, Archbishop of Canterbury from 1896 to 1902. Both men, along with Alfred Zimmern, were part of the 'Catiline Club' which met weekly for lunch. The conspirators were all either Liberal or Labour and by this time the young Livingstone had thrown over his parents' Toryism for the Liberal party. Their campaign for reform reached a climax in April, 1907, with a series of articles in *The Times* under the heading, 'Oxford and the Nation'.*

The dons were able to interest the Chancellor, Lord Curzon, who drew up his own proposals which he published in 1909. In time there was a Royal Commission (which reported in 1922) and certain changes were made. *The Times*, looking back after fifty years, wrote 'If Oxford is today no more "the playground of the idle rich" and has a faculty organisation and arrangements for postgraduate study which compare favourably with those of other seats of learning. . .this is due in no small measure to the group of earnest and (as it was then thought) impertinent young men among whom Livingstone and William Temple. . .were leading spirits.'†

University politics were only one aspect of his life. Livingstone was a popular tutor and in 1912 he brought out his first book, *The Greek Genius and Its Meaning to Us*. In this he first expounded his view (as had Gilbert Murray before him) that Classical thought was not a dead academic subject but a living entity.

In the following year he married Cecil Maryon-Wilson and in time they would have four children, two sons and two daughters. He stayed at Corpus during the Great War except for one year (1917–1918) when he taught at Eton. In 1916 he brought out another book on the theme which would largely dominate his life, *A Defence of Classical Education*, and in 1920 he was a member of the Prime Minister's Committee on the Classics: one assumes the committee had the patronage of the Prime Minister but little more as Lloyd George, whatever his merits as a politican and Welsh orator, had little interest in classical learning. Also in 1920 Livingstone became joint editor of the *Classical Review*, a position he held until 1922.

In the years to come there was a constant stream of books, editions and translations, a full list of which is given in the Appendix. One of his most important scholarly achievements was to originate and act as general editor of the Clarendon Series which published classical texts with both the original and a translation included. His scholarship, editing and writing were earning him a considerable reputation. One American student, Alan Valentine, later President of Stanford University, was at the university in the 1920s and later wrote of the challenges placed before an American student by studying at Oxford: 'The cultural ideals of Matthew Arnold or Richard Livingstone do not merge comfortably with those of Hollywood, the *Daily Mirror*, or *Time Magazine*.'*

In 1924 Livingstone accepted the position as Vice-Chancellor of the Queen's University, Belfast. When he arrived in Ulster, he found that the University had wide support throughout the

Province and occupied a unique position among British universities, being regarded as the 'university of a people'. He also found that it was seriously handicapped by lack of funds. Instead of demanding increased government support the new Vice-Chancellor campaigned for more support from within the Province, pointing out that people should take on more responsibility for 'their' university. He established a University Guild to bridge that peculiarly British disease, the division between 'town' and 'gown' and in time the Guild helped in financing the University. Livingstone was also active in various schemes to improve life in Belfast, particularly with regard to health. In 1931 he received the accolade of knighthood from King George V in recognition of his achievements and two years later, in 1933, Sir Richard returned to Oxford to become President of his old College, a position he would hold until retirement in 1950.

Back at Oxford, Livingstone combined his classical scholarship with work for educational reform. He was a member of the Committee for Social Studies when this field was being developed with assistance from the Rockefeller Foundation, which was to prove such a friend to Oxford over the years. In 1936 he was President of the Education Section of the British Association and throughout the 1930s he was in frequent demand as a speaker and broadcaster. In 1937-1938 he advocated the first 'summer school' for colonial administrators from the Empire: he wanted the idea developed so that Oxford could share her resources with those responsible for improving the lives of the people committed to their care. He looked to the new Nuffield College for assistance in this work but was disappointed. In 1938 he served as President of the Hellenic Society and in 1940-1 as President of the Classical Association.

When the war came he was anxious to contribute his share to the heightened debate over education which marked the war years and resulted, in part, in the 1944 Education Act. In 1941 he spelled out his views in *The Future in Education* in the Cambridge University Press' 'Current Problems' series, edited by his friend Sir Ernest Barker. The series discussed a wide range of topics, from political propaganda, military strategy and foreign relations, to the colonies, public schools, India, and Christianity. Livingstone's book, the sixth in the series, was a great success, partly because his arguments were set forth 'with the distinction and the persuasive simplicity of which Livingstone was such a master'. He argued against raising the school leaving age to sixteen and in favour of more part-time education for fourteen to eighteen year olds. He wanted to transform public schools by subjecting them to public control and by admitting only boys of proven ability and he wanted a large development of adult education along the lines of what was done in Denmark. His motto was 'adult education for the educated'. He was overwhelmed with invitations to develop his ideas in talks and articles.

In 1943 he enlarged his contribution to the debate by publishing, in the same Cambridge series, *Education for a World Adrift*: simply to expand educational opportunities and to reform existing structures were not enough. Indeed, all the activity this could bring about might hide the real question: how good was the education being expanded?

Although at Corpus he was seen by many as a shrewd administrator and a dignified scholar, his time as Vice Chancellor (1944-1947) was not a success. At that time the Vice Chancellorship moved every three years to succeeding heads of houses in a settled rota. With the end of the war and the return of so many demobilised soldiers, it would not have been an easy time for any Vice Chancellor. The *Dictionary of National Biography* simply says that he 'failed to gain the full confidence of the University'. In the event he created a controversy when he suggested that the Vice Chancellorship should become a permanent position: his proposal was rejected by Congregation, the University's parliament. A modified proposal, which would have allowed the Chancellor to appoint the Vice Chancellor, was also rejected. (It would have been some comfort for Livingstone to know that in time the University would alter its rules so that the Vice Chancellor no longer automatically comes from the heads of houses but is elected and that candidates other than heads of houses can stand.)

After his term of office ended in 1947 Sir Richard stayed on for another three years as President of Corpus Christi College. In 1948 he opened Denman College, the Women's Institutes' residential college. The college, named after the first Chairman of the National Federation of Women's Institutes, Lady Denman, was at Marcham in Oxfordshire and owed much to Livingstone's inspiration. A lecture room was named after him and a bust from life by Kathleen Parbury was placed in the garden. Then, in 1950, at the age of seventy, he retired as President of Corpus. A portrait, by Eric Kennington, hangs in the hall.

His retirement brought him little rest as he was in constant demand as a lecturer and broadcaster, especially in Canada and the United States where his reputation was, if anything, greater than in Britain. He was honoured by the Universities of Cambridge, Belfast, Toronto, Durham, Manchester, London, Columbia, Yale, St Andrews and Dublin and he received from Norway the King Haakon VII Liberty Cross, from France the Legion d'Honneur and from Greece the Order of King George I. In Oxford he earned immortal fame as the subject of an undergraduate joke still extant: a young man, seeking to enter Corpus after the gate had been closed, chose a window. Unfortunately the window opened into the bedroom of Sir Richard and Lady Livingstone. After the intruder awoke them and Lady Livingstone evidenced her alarm, the undergraduate bowed and said with the sang-froid natural to Oxonians, 'Lady Livingstone, I presume.' His charm earned him a complete pardon.

Sir Richard died on 26 December, 1960. Seven years later the Italian scholar, Giacinto Grassi, published in the *Eductori Antichi e Moderni* series his study, *Richard Livingstone*. The book was published in Florence, the city where just under six hundred years before, the Byzantine diplomat, Chrysoloras, settled to teach Greek to the European barbarians and to open to them the works of Aristotle and Plato, Aeschelus and Euripedes.

The Times in an obituary, which ran to two long columes,

said, 'By his death this country loses one of its leading Greek scholars and the most active champion of classical studies.' It went on to describe him as a 'Greek Scholar and Humanist'. The *Dictionary of National Biography* described him as an 'educationalist'. Both were correct: Classical scholarship, liberal humanism in the sense inherited from the Renaissance and education, especially education of as high a quality as possible for as many as possible: all were the hall-marks and life work of Sir Richard Livingstone. All three strains in his character run through the whole of *Education for a World Adrift*. Although written in the dark days of the last War, when Great Britain, her Empire and Commonwealth along with the United States defended Christian civilisation against the combined evils of German nazism and Japanese cruelty, the book remains as pertinent as ever.

Indeed, Sir Richard Livingstone's message is more relevant now than it was in the 1940s. He stands today as a prophet who does not make predictions for the future but recalls us to the truths of the past, of our history and make-up as a people, of our Christian heritage — truths we have been encouraged by forces, sometimes opportunist, sometimes downright evil, to forget. If his message has a ring of 'Victorian values' about it, it is because the Victorians were the last generation of Englishmen unashamedly to prefer reality to rhetoric. They sought to take man as he was (as opposed to how we should prefer him) and to improve on what they found. To those who know no standards but those of their own making or of their generation's making, this book will come as a shock: so be it.

We have extended educational opportunities, we have built more schools and universities, we have reduced class sizes, we have hired more teachers, we have published more books and we have restructured education as frequently almost as we have elected new governments: but have we actually improved the education we give our children? Have we not, perhaps, lost the very foundation of that education by losing its Christian basis? Have we not dreamt in T. S. Eliot's words of 'systems so perfect that no one will need to be good'?*

Concerning the knowledge necessary to living Sir Richard wrote, 'But of this all-important side of education — doubly important in a world of shaken beliefs and uncertain values — we hear very little'. Sir Richard continues,

> Knowledge is important, still more so is the power to use it; but most important of all is what a man believes, what he thinks good and bad, whether he has clear values and standards and is prepared to live by them. Paradox as it may sound, this matters more to the making of a new world, and to its preservation, even than equality of opportunity.

What Sir Richard, a twentieth century teacher grounded in the sure values of the past and trying to ensure that these values should continue to guide our ways, would not have believed is that British society could so change that whole sections of the intelligentsia — teachers, journalists, writers, clergymen and bishops — could reject wholesale the very idea that we exist in a context inherited from our ancestors, that we live, not in their steps but in their country. We may call Sir Richard's view 'vertical' — he looked forward to a world at peace and a country extending her riches to all her people; he looked backward to the past for guidance from those who had gone before.

We may call the newer view 'horizontal': it recognises no past, it is existential in its belief that our generation, unlike any before, stands alone, without roots or limits. This new, a-historical view looks to sociology and anthropology and goes under many names. Children are taught not that they live in England or Wales or Scotland or Ireland but in 'societies' made up of 'communities' of self-styled groups: 'gays', 'feminists' and even the odd old-fashioned Englishman stuck in for good measure. There is no unity claimed and no boundary recognised: we all just happen to live on the same island. Some have lived here for millenia; others have just arrived, bringing with them religions from the east. In the new view traditional English 'tolerance' must be re-placed by a worship of anything that is new and alien. If nothing is universally recognised as being right, nothing can be condemned as wrong. If we have no belief, at least none inherited from the past, we are become, in T. S. Eliot's words, soulless 'societies' in which 'We all dwell together to make money from each other'.*

This new religion is often called 'multi-faith', that is, no faith. The truly amazing thing is that the churches' leadership, especially the Bishops of the Church of England, in a never-ending and never successful attempt to win the approval of the intelligentsia who serve at the altars of the new religion, preach not 'Christ crucified' but the new, 'multi-faith Britain'. The professional doubters, living off the wealth of lands and gifts left to the church by the faithful whose faith they now deny in episcopal palace and Oxbridge common room, attack the very essence of Christian belief. This is, of course, nothing new: heretics are not an invention of the twentieth century and episcopal heretics go back as far as the episcopacy. The writer, H. H. Munro (Saki), has one character in his novel, *The Unbearable Bassington* say, 'My dear Archdeacon. . .no one can be an unbeliever nowadays. The Christian Apologists have left one nothing to disbelieve.' That was written in 1912.†

The type of a-historical desert, with no history, no great men and no inherited values is seen in those schools under the control of Local Education Authorities dominated by what we now call the 'loony left'. A teacher at Bristol's 'Multicultural Educational Centre', hardly a hotbed of Tory reaction, was accused of the sin of 'racism' because he attempted to teach immigrant children the English language. To teach English in 'multi-cultural Britain' is to assert that it is a 'better' language than those brought by the immigrants. In the London Borough of Brent the socialist controlled council introduced on 1 October 1986 the country's first 'multi-faith religious syllabus' which treats all religions as if they were 'equal'. The Christian faith was mentioned once, in an appendix.

The chairman of the committee responsible for the 'syllabus' was an ordained priest of the Church of England, the Revd Roger Mason who told *The Times* that 'we must adapt to local conditions'. However the paper discovered that Mr. Mason's three children were sent not to local 'multi-faith schools' but out of Brent, to a Church school in Westminster. Presumably other Englishmen living in Brent had no such choice. One wonders how the reverend gentleman could square this with his ordination promise, 'to banish and drive away all erroneous and strange doctrines contrary to God's word'. Sadly, the examples of these local deserts are far too numerous to mention here.†

The future of a post-Christian Britain in which the ever-busy zealots of this 'new world' were at work was foreseen by T. S. Eliot in *The Idea of a Christian Society*. 'We might, of course, merely sink into an apathetic decline' he wrote,

> . . .without faith, and therefore without faith in ourselves; without a philosophy of life, either Christian or pagan; and without art. Or we might get a 'Totalitarian democracy', different but having much in common with other pagan societies, because we shall have changed step by step in order to keep pace with them: a state of affairs in which we shall have regimentation and conformity, without respect for the needs of the individual soul. . .uniformity of opinion through propaganda. . .

Eliot, along with C. S. Lewis and Sir Richard Livingstone saw what would replace a society based on the Christian faith would be not just pagan indifference but a new religion and this is exactly what is being offered our children. What Eliot, Lewis or Livingstone could never have fully seen was that the churches, afraid of meeting the real challenge set before them, funked the issue and opted for the soft option of aiding the new faith to establish itself.*

Sir Richard confined himself mainly to education because this was where he could speak with authority and he foresaw that it was in education that the battle would be fought. In this he was absolutely correct. Sociologists of education (those who make a living by talking about teaching) are today often in the vanguard of an anti-Christian crusade, partly in the deluded belief that their 'professional integrity' is lessened by 'teaching Christianity'. They are silently abetted by those, a very large number, who imagine that a moral code based on 'Christian values' and with which they are comfortable, can outlast the

Christian faith which gave that 'code' to the world. Livingstone saw through this ruse:

> . . .we are living on character formed in the past by beliefs which are now shaken or destroyed. Character takes long to form, but it is not quickly destroyed. . .A plant may continue in apparent health for some time after its roots have been cut, yet its days are numbered. The case of Germany witnesses to the truth of this contention. Who, thirty years ago, would have believed a prophet who said that a decent, friendly, highly educated and civilised people, among whom Christianity was apparently still strong, would be capable of the persecution of the Jews, the horrors of the concentration camps, the barbarism. . .The spiritual roots of Germany had been cut, and rootless virtues are precarious. But how strong are the roots of *our* virtues?. . .Those who reject Christian beliefs, cannot count on keeping Christian morals.

Livingstone went on to remind those who like morality but dislike 'dogma' that 'To say that the teaching of Jesus, or any of it, conveys the truth about life, is a highly dogmatic statement, implying a very definite view about the universe and human nature; to say that the teaching is false or valueless is equally dogmatic; and it is also dogmatic to say that we cannot form an opinion on the matter but must suspend our judgment.' He reminded those who pretended (and still pretend) to some type of intellectual superiority because they are 'above' Christian faith, 'there is no credit, least of all any intellectual credit, in halting between two opinions, when in fact you must *act* as if one or the other was true.' Surely the rise in crimes against the individual, especially women, and the increasing acts of vandalism which mar the English townscape expose the argument that morals can long outlive faith. For increasing numbers of young people, what can be the ultimate sanction for their moral behaviour? Will it be social concensus? or just private sentiment? What guarantee is there that it will not be eroded in its turn, once faith has totally disappeared? Like long division we shall be left with a remainder too small to pass on.

The battle ground was education and this is why throughout

his numerous writings on the subject, Sir Richard Livingstone never tired in insisting that the purpose of education was not the mere accumulation of facts or the successful sitting of examinations, but the creation of character to ensure a truly civilised society. To men like Livingstone this was a birth-right of every school-child and was not to be thrown away for a pottage of 'multi-cultural' nonsense. The quality of any civilisation, Livingstone insists, 'depends on its standards, its sense of values, its idea of what is first-rate and what is not.' The importance of character, to men like Livingstone, meant learning how to live life by studying those who have gone before us, not just individual men and women of our own country but of other civilisations which have contributed to the making of our own.

This naturally led men of Livingstone's generation to turn to Greece and Rome as today it leads some others to turn to Africa or Asia for examples in 'community politics'. The highlands of Illyria were to him more important than the delta of the Ganges. Sir Richard's greatest love, which inspired his devotion to education, was for the Classics and especially Plato. Throughout *Education for a World Adrift* he turns again and again to the Greeks, and especially to Plato, for answers and illustrations. To Sir Richard our cultural and political origins, if not our religion, began with Hellenic culture and Christianity itself was nutured in Greek thought. Thankfully he did not live long enough to see the virtual disappearance of the Classics not just from schools but from the ancient universities. Yet he was no academic snob, demanding that educated men must speak Greek or Latin when English would do perfectly well. Translations (on which he worked throughout his long life) could enable all to read and benefit from Hellenic literature, to see that the values we hold could be traced back not just to Christian revelation but to natural law and man's very nature.

Sir Richard Livingstone's devotion to Classical learning carried into the 1940s and '50s a tradition that had begun late in the fourteenth century and first blossomed in fifteenth century Italy. Just as Lorenzo Valla had translated

Thucydides for Pope Nicholas so Livingstone, five centuries later, edited selections from the same Greek historian for Oxford University Press in the same year in which *Education for a World Adrift* was published. In his Preface to that translation he wrote, 'It is part of a liberal education to know the greatest things in the world. . .' and this was the key to his love for the Classics. No civilised man could simply walk past a monument and not wonder at its significance; the writings of Plato, Horace, Tacitus, Pliny, Aristotle, Thucydides, Plutarch, Sophocles, Euripides, Homer, Aristophanes, Cicero, Menander, Protagoras, Aeschylus, Virgil or Marcus Aurelius were as much an Englishman's heritage as those of Milton, Shakespeare or Tennyson.*

This tradition has not completely died out. Last September the Prince of Wales, while speaking at Harvard University's 350th Commemoration Ceremony, told his audience:

> I would suggest that we have been gradually losing sight of the Greek philosophers' ideal, which was to produce a balance between the several subjects that catered for a boy's moral, intellectual, emotional and physical needs. While we have been right to demand the kind of technical education relevant to the needs of the twentieth century, it would appear that we may have forgotten that when all is said and done a good man, as the Greeks would say, is a nobler work than a good technologist. We should never lose sight of the fact that to avert disaster we have not only to teach men to make things, but also to produce people who have complete moral control over the things they make.†

Only a few months before, the Lord Chancellor, Lord Hailsham, spoke at the centenary of the British School of Archaeology in Athens and referred to the 'immense debt of gratitude which every civilised European, I would add every percipient Christian, owes to this beautiful country, and to the genius of her sons and daughters, their passion for freedom, their φιλοξενία [hospitality to strangers], their love of the beautiful. They were the true architects of European culture. . In Hellas Europe was born. . .If', Lord Hailsham added, 'the muezzin does not now sound on Ludgate Hill instead of the bells of St Paul's, we must recognise that this is largely due to the martial courage and skills of the Byzantine Emperors and their troops who held the gates of Europe just long enough to civilise our own coarse and sometimes brutal ancestors'. As Livingstone argues, 'A man may know nothing of Greek thought and literature; he may be an agnostic or an atheist; but Greece, Rome and Christianity have made Western Civilisation, permeate its thoughts, morals, literature and institutions, and touch its members at every moment of their lives.'*

Throughout his life Livingstone never wavered in his struggle to remind his countrymen of the debt they owed Hellenic and Roman culture. In his first book, *The Greek Genius and Its Meaning to Us,* published in 1912, he wrote that Attica 'has given us an art which we, with it and all that the world has done since it for our models, have equalled perhaps, but not surpassed. It has given us the staple of our vocabulary in every domain of thought and knowledge'. The young Richard Livingstone reminded his readers that the Greek was

> . . .no more a Mid-Victorian aesthete than he was a Cobdenite Liberal. His real peculiarity was an overpowering energy, that was always busy at something. With a childish delight he threw himself on the world that opened before him, travelling, trading, prospecting, fighting, founding small settlements. . .an elector, a voter, an administrator, a public servant, yet not too busy for recreation or religion when the calendar brought the feast-day round, and taking art and literature as two among the thousand occupations of his kaleidoscopic life.'†

Livingstone admired Greek education because it aimed at producing students knowledgeable in their own culture and equipped to lead society, not students trained at passing examinations and qualified in one, or, at best, two narrow fields with no philosophy of life to guide them and no understanding of their own culture — skilled technocrats and nothing more. That is not education, he argues. His definition is as follows:

> The healthy human being, finding himself a creature of unknown

capacities in an unknown world, wants to learn what the world is like, and what he should be and do in it. To help him in answering these questions is the one and only purpose of education. . .the examination system is a poison which slows down education in most cases and in some paralyses it, and no one wholly escapes its bad effects.

At the heart of any sound education lay the question of morality, of 'standards, right values, the science of good and evil. . .To implant these is an essential part of education' and Livingstone quotes Bishop Berkeley who wrote, 'he who hath not much meditated upon God, the Humane mind, and the *Summum bonum*, may possibly make a thriving earthworm, but will certainly make a sorry patriot and a sorry statesman.'*

This edition of *Education for a World Adrift*, Number 17 in the 'Current Problems' series published by Cambridge University Press, is based on the first edition, published in February 1943. The text is as published and any additional editorial material has been confined to the Notes at the end.

Sir Richard's own notes have been expanded and corrected where necessary and are included in the Notes as published here. His own comments are printed in italic. So that the reader who does not wish to consult the Notes may not be hampered in his reading, the Notes are only indicated by an asterisk or dagger (if there are more than two notes per page) at the end of the paragraph in which the note occurs. Works cited in the Editor's Introduction are found at the beginning of the Notes.

The Appendix contains a list of works written, translated or edited by Sir Richard Livingstone.

The Editor would like to express his appreciation to H.R.H. the Prince of Wales for permission to read and to quote from his address given before Harvard University on the occasion of the University's 350th Commemoration on 4 September 1986 and to the Rt Hon. the Lord Chancellor, Lord Hailsham, C.H., F.R.S., D.C.L. for permission to read and to quote from his speech to the British School of Archaeology at Athens on 20 June 1986.

He would also wish to express his gratitude to the Hon. E.R.H. Wills and The Farmington Trust for the assistance given in the preparation of this edition. It was Mr Wills who first saw the need to re-publish this book and supported the project with his customary generous enthusiasm. The editor would also wish to thank Mr Desmond Sullivan for his encouragement and assistance in this work, and Dr R. F. Mullen, Col R.J.A. Hornby, O.B.E., Mr Peter Gray, Mr Roger Shone, Miss Priscilla Tolkien, Mrs Caroline White, Mr D. Mack Smith of All Souls College, Oxford, and Miss Richenda Buxton, the Rights Manager at Cambridge University Press, for their help.

Oxford
6 June, 1987.

J.E.B. Munson

PREFACE TO THE FIRST EDITION

ENGLAND has probably never been so interested in education as to-day. There are many reasons: the obvious and increasing importance of knowledge to life; a sense of the great possibilities of modern civilisation and of its disorders and dangers; the perception that our democracy is very ill-educated; a realisation that in foreign politics between 1919 and 1939 we have thrown away a great victory with a rapidity and completeness perhaps unexampled in history and that this has been partly due to political ignorance; the need of extending education if equality of opportunity is to be more than a phrase. These considerations have interested all classes in education and forced it into the foreground. So everyone is talking about the subject, our educational system is being reviewed, and a great development of it is imminent. All this is to the good; the tide is setting in strongly and may carry us far up the shore of our need and desire. But it will not do so unless we have the right education as well as the right educational system, and we sometimes forget that these are different, though related, things.

Much of the present interest in education is political or social rather than educational. I was speaking recently about education to a large working-class audience. Their keenness was inspiring, their criticism acute and searching. But their interest was wholly in one side of the problem; in the provision of proper educational facilities, in equality of opportunity, in securing a fair chance to every child, irrespective of the position or means of its parents. They wanted more education, but did not ask what it was to teach. They were deeply concerned about the residential school, but concerned that the poor should have the same access to it as the well-to-do and not with its educational merits or defects. Their interest was in no sense mercenary; they were not thinking of education as a road to better-paid jobs: they wanted fair play for all, and they were anxious to get the educational system which would achieve this.

This attitude is natural and right. In an age of social change and in a society like our own where opportunity has hitherto not been equal, the problem of equal opportunity demands to be solved and rightly fills the mind. But there is a danger that it may overfill it, engross the attention with educational machinery and make us so concerned with providing schools that we do not consider what is to be taught inside them. Machinery is indispensable to education, but when it has been provided the bigger problem of education remains and begins. What are we to teach? At what should our education aim? What sort of human beings should it produce? These questions might interest us more.

The knowledge necessary to living must be imparted. People must be taught to use their brains. We are aware of both these needs. But there is something still more essential to which less attention is paid. Knowledge is important, still more so is the power to use it; but most important of all is what a man believes, what he thinks good and bad, whether he has clear values and standards and is prepared to live by them. Paradox as it may sound, this matters more to the making of a new world, and to its preservation, even than equality of opportunity. But of this all-important side of education—doubly important in a world of shaken beliefs and uncertain values—we hear very little. Speeches, conferences, the educational press are more occupied with educational machinery than with education. Nursery schools, raising of the school age, part-time continued education, adult study—these fill the papers, and are essential, but are not enough. As Plato said, the noblest of all studies is the study of what man should be and how he should live. It is also the most important of all studies: do we give it enough attention?

Every age has a blind eye and sees nothing wrong in practices and institutions which its successors view with just horror. The eighteenth century complacently accepted the penal laws; we have only recently discovered the absurdity and injustice of leaving three-quarters of the population without any education after the age of 14. Perhaps our grandchildren, amazed at abuses and errors which we do not notice, may say of us: 'How blind that generation was to its real problem—the human being! They boasted that science had unified the world. So indeed it had, with the result that German submarines could sink ships off the coasts of America, that wireless could carry propaganda to any country in any continent, and that men were looking forward to the day when aircraft could bomb New York from Europe and Europe from New York. They never saw that the only real unity is spiritual and that however great the advantage of being able to cross the Atlantic in eight hours, co-operation depends not on rapid transport, but on common ideals. They were conscious of the defects in their commercial and industrial system, but though their standards and values were far more chaotic, they did nothing to remedy the chaos. So their peace-time civilisation was both impressive and depressing; the unlimited means at their disposal were largely misused. Their education did little to help them. It was like a half-assembled motorcar; most of the parts were there, but they were not put together. Reformers wished to base it on science and technology, or on sociology and economics, whose importance they saw; if they had had their way, they would have produced a good chassis, but overlooked the need of an engine—not to speak of a driver who knew where to go. The real problem lay deeper than science or sociology or politics; it was spiritual. They were dimly aware of it, but, in the English way, they averted their eyes from a difficult and embarrassing question; as some sufferers from cancer avoid consulting a doctor till it is too late. It is not surprising that in the end war tore their civilisation to pieces.' There would be some justice in such a comment.

We have fine material to work on—a good racial stock, a sound national character hammered out through a thousand years on the anvil of history. In the past, spiritual forces, of which Christianity is the chief, have done much to control and direct the country, but these forces, which at all times fight an uphill battle, have lost ground; and in proportion as they lose it, life loses direction and purpose, and character becomes a habit whose roots are dead, a house whose foundations are sapped. Here is our biggest need; the need of values and standards which are more than mere habits, which go down below the soil of custom into the rock of clear conviction and are founded in a philosophy of life. The English have never been fond of the idea of anything that could be called a philosophy; they have their virtues and are content with them. But ultimately virtues depend on beliefs, and though sound habits are admirable, it is dangerous to rely on them in an age of change. Our real problem lies deeper than politics, science or economics, and in the absence of a spiritual ideal we shall never solve it. If we go on as at present, we shall probably decline into an economic religion, worshipping material prosperity in a more or less refined form. Such a religion is inglorious and, because it does not satisfy the deeper needs of human nature, short-lived.

This book attempts to raise the problem, discussing its nature (Chapter I)—how far our education deals with it (Chapter II)—the use of history and literature in forming values and standards (Chapter III)—the basis of a spiritual philosophy of life (Chapter IV). Chapter V deals with the obstacles presented by the examination system and over-specialisation; Chapter VI, with education for citizenship. I have had higher education primarily in mind, and have assumed that in the future every citizen will receive this through part-time and adult education if not otherwise; but clearly much of what is here said applies *mutatis mutandis* to elementary education.

The last chapter was delivered as the Seth Memorial Lecture at Edinburgh University and parts of the first as the Aneurin Williams Memorial Lecture. Some passages in the book appeared in an article in *The Round Table*. Professor Ernest Barker and Sir Alfred Zimmern read the book in typescript and helped me with valuable suggestions. R.L. *Dec. 1942*

δεῖ μανθάνειν καὶ συνεθίζεσθαι μηδὲν οὕτως ὡς τὸ κρίνειν ὀρθῶς καὶ χαίρειν τοῖς ἐπιεικέσιν ἤθεσι καὶ ταῖς καλαῖς πράξεσιν.

Aristotle, *Politics* VIII. 5. 17.

No lesson is so important to learn, and no habit is so important to acquire, as a right judgment and a delight in fine characters and noble actions.

EDUCATION FOR A WORLD ADRIFT

CHAPTER I

THE PROBLEM

A RIVER is always flowing; over most of its reaches the flow is so slow and peaceful that the direction of the current can hardly be discerned and may even be mistaken, but at times the stream bed falls rapidly and it hurries in a turmoil of broken water. As with rivers, so with the individual; change is always taking place, but only at certain periods of life can it be clearly perceived. There are times when a human being alters quickly and perceptibly: we met him one summer and he was much the same as when we saw him last. We meet him six months later and he has undergone a visible change; he has grown up, we say, or matured, or developed, or become old; he has become a different being, or he is not the man he was. So too with the State. It is always changing, for the most part imperceptibly. You cannot, as Heraclitus said, step twice into the same river: nor is England or any of us quite what we were a year ago. But there come times when the nature or the pace of change is such that no one can mistake it. It is the fate of this generation to live in such an age. England in the next ten or twenty years will become a very different country from what it was yesterday, even from what it is to-day.

If you ask me what this change is, I should say that it is the decisive appearance of a new character on the stage: a new class is taking a main rôle in the play. Our generation is seeing the same kind of phenomenon as occurred in the fifteenth, the seventeenth and the nineteenth centuries—a radical change.

At the close of the fifteenth century the monarch achieved a domination which lasted some hundred years; in the seventeenth century, after a moment when it seemed as if something like English democracy might be established, power passed into the hands of an upper class; with the Reform Bill the middle classes took control; to-day it is the turn of what we compendiously call 'the masses', and government of the people, for the people, is in sight, if not here. It is not an isolated phenomenon; such a change belongs to the spirit of the age; it can be seen in the Russian revolution, and it is bound to come in all educated countries. For fundamentally it is the result of education. Marx would have traced it to economic causes, and doubtless these have contributed. But the real cause is education. As soon as you begin to educate people, you teach them, however feebly, to use their reason. The more intelligent can use it effectively, the less intelligent will at any rate have an idea what the more intelligent are saying. And as soon as people begin to think, they will among other questions ask themselves: 'Why should there be such inequalities in life; in particular why should the children of some people have inadequate food, living conditions, education, etc., while the children of others, whatever their brains or character, have secure access not only to the necessities of a good life but to the superfluities of a luxurious one?' As soon as this simple question is asked by a sufficient number of people, social change begins; it is the lever which has set change in motion to-day. The answer is infinitely less simple than the question; summary solutions to the problem would only aggravate it and leave the world far worse off than it is. I do not know a solution and shall not attempt to suggest one. I merely wish to emphasise that Britain is going through a period of social and political change as great and difficult as it went through at the Reformation and in the seventeenth century and in the period of the Industrial Revolution and the Reform Bill.

The adventurous, the romantic, the heroic can count themselves fortunate to live at such a time; they are not born out of due season; the time may be out of joint but they will never say

> O cursed spite
> That ever we were born to set it right.*

The majority, in whose nature these qualitites are less richly mixed, may regret that they were not born earlier or later, but they may feel that this is a situation to which the words apply which Socrates used of life, καλὸν τὸ ἆθλον καὶ ἡ ἔλπις μεγάλη—'noble is the prize and our hope is great'.

Our hope is great, for the country has been through such storms before and has survived them. There were times in the sixteenth and the seventeenth and the early nineteenth centuries when things looked far darker. And the prize is a noble one. We have a great task and a great opportunity. Our revolution will not bring the millennium, which is the Mrs Harris of politicians—constantly appealed to but never seen. It may alter England for the worse; for such changes must shake and may destroy existing traditions and values, but fail to replace them by better ones. In any case, it will have drawbacks, defects and losses to set against gains. But an alteration in the balance of English life is as inevitable now as it was in the days of the Reform Bill; it has been proceeding for the last thirty years and must be completed; and it is just. Our business is to see it is carried out in the spirit of justice—not as a competition between the selfishness of the rich and the selfishness of the poor, but as an attempt to create a better civilisation. The prize is noble. This ship of Britain carries a crew of more than forty million human beings whose future depends on the issue of the voyage, and a freight of ideals, traditions, virtues, which have enriched humanity in the past and have not lost their power or use. If we weather the storm, not only shall we preserve the ship for new voyages of wider range, but we may again teach the world the greatest of political lessons—how to carry out a revolution without bloodshed or injustice, with a minimum of hardship and a maximum of gain. In Pitt's words, we may save ourselves by our exertions and Europe by our example.*

The task facing us has two sides, different though interdependent. We have to build a house for the new world to inhabit, to create the framework of material civilisation, which social and political changes require and which the new knowledge puts at our command. It is an age of science and applied science and we must make full use of them. Therefore, to profit by our opportunity, it is essential that we should have enough scientists and technologists, and equally necessary that our politicians, civil servants, business men and general public should appreciate the value and uses of science. (This is different from being actually trained in science, though it is generally confused with it; because a nation needs a sufficient supply of chemists and physicists, it does not mean that we should all be physicists and chemists.) Nor is it only scientists and awareness of science that we need. Economics, administration, foreign policy, social organisation, cannot be left to the half knowledge and bright ideas of the amateur, as they were so largely left in the last century. The foundation of the Royal Institute of International Affairs is a witness to our need; it is surprising that the need for it was not realised till 1919; and it is even more surprising that there is nothing comparable to it for the study of Social and Political Science and that these studies should still be comparatively unorganised. When we come to provide the political, social and industrial machinery necessary, if the society of to-morrow is to express itself and function efficiently, we are likely to regret not having made systematic provision for its study: we shall be in the position of an army that takes the field without a General Staff. Expert knowledge is the obvious need of our infinitely complicated hive. So much is generally agreed; and there most people would stop. Enough science, enough economics, enough sociology, and the hive will settle down to an era of abundant and increasing honey. It might, if we were bees and not creatures of far more irrational and stormy passions, uncontrolled by mere knowledge, unsatisfied by honeycombs however full.*

Our task has another side which is even more important. There is no better summary of the problem of society than nine Greek words, which in English can be translated: 'The State comes into existence for the sake of life, it exists for the sake of good life.' This clear and simple analysis of the problem is characteristically Greek, and we should do well continually to bear it in mind and not, in our legitimate efforts to secure what Aristotle calls 'life', forget that the State 'exists for the sake of the good life'. That elementary fact is easily ignored. 'New orders' are apt to have an economic bias. But it is possible to achieve peace, material prosperity, and abolition of unemployment, and yet have a civilisation of little value: as we are reminded by Mr T. S. Eliot's epitaph on our comfortable suburbs:

> A Cry from the North, from the West and from the South:
> Whence thousands travel daily to the timekept City,
> Where My Word is unspoken.
> In the land of lobelias and tennis flannels
> The rabbit shall burrow and the thorn revisit,
> The nettle shall flourish on the gravel court,
> And the wind shall say: 'Here were decent godless people:
> Their only monument the asphalt road
> And a thousand lost golf balls.'†

Here the spread of democracy will not necessarily help us; indeed it makes our task more difficult. To call the masses into power is to dilute existing culture. They must be humoured and satisfied; attention must be paid to their interests and tastes, and if these are trifling, ignoble and base, the level of civilisation will fall. There is good democracy: there is also the democracy which Mussolini described as 'a social order in which a degenerate mass has no other care than to enjoy the ignoble pleasures of vulgar men'; as it was said of the masses under the Roman Empire that 'the once sovereign people has thrown its cares to the winds, limits its ambitions and only asks anxiously for two things, bread and the games of the Circus'. It is easy to translate *panem et Circenses* into modern equivalents—free bread and free amusements, doles and the dogs. The spread of democracy may mean cultural decline. Plato said: 'Political constitutions are made not from wood and stone but from the dispositions of their citizens, which turn the scale and draw everything in their wake', and already we have seen the influence of the masses drawing our civilisation in their wake. The newspapers of to-day with the biggest circulation are on a lower level than any published fifty years ago. In the last century there were no football pools, no nation-wide organisation of betting, no litter nuisance; the drama may have been poor, but it did not fall so low as most films of our time. Do not blame the masses for this; blame the newspaper proprietors, the film magnates, the organisers of pools; and let us blame ourselves, who have left the masses without the higher education which might have given them an antidote to the poison. We have called a new class on to the stage, but done little to prepare it for its rôle.*

The clearest condemnation of our pre-war civilisation is that though the war has destroyed much of it, we have little to regret except some beautiful buildings, and are a better people leading better lives than in peace. If our civilisation disappeared utterly, and archaeologists excavating our rubbish heaps 1000 years hence had to reconstruct it from the remains of the cheap newspapers, films and advertisements, which reflect the amusements and desires of most of the population, they would probably class the pre-war world with the decadence of the Roman Empire. Comparing us with the Middle Ages which built cathedrals and churches, they would label the twentieth century 'the cinema-building age'. If the reviews of novels in that admirable paper *The Times Literary Supplement* had survived to show the tastes of the educated class, the future historian would be surprised at a society apparently interested by a succession of sex adventures, books on Byron's 'loves' and biographies of the major and minor courtesans of history: he might suppose that, though presumably all of our novelists had read Shakespeare and some had read Homer, many of them found their ideal of woman in the unchaste maidservants of Odysseus rather than in Nausicaa and Penelope, in Cressida and Helen rather than in Portia or Beatrice: and he might head his chapter on pre-war novels with the contemptuous comment of Thersites in *Troilus and Cressida*: 'What's become of the wenching rogues?...But in a sort lechery eats itself.' Certainly he would wonder that Shakespeare's nation produced so many writers who were without his sense of good and evil; and ask why, in the crisis of European civilisation, the intellectuals ridiculed, denounced or deplored the weaknesses of their time but had not the faith or constructive power to see a vision of better things that might have renewed it.*

No doubt I am putting one side of the case. But it is a very important side. If we were looking for a catchword to describe our age, various phrases would occur to the mind: we might call it the Age of Science, or the Age of Social Revolution, or the Age without Standards. None would be exhaustive, none quite just; but the last would have some claim to consideration. That may seem a hard judgment. For our age has great virtues; they were present in peace, they have been revealed to the world and to ourselves by the war. Our weakness is that good and evil are mixed together and that the tares not only grow among the wheat but are not distinguished from it. Look at any issue of our cheap daily papers in peace-time and you will see what I mean; or take an instance from *Life*, a journal which has excellent and serious articles in it, and then, among all this first-rate matter, the following description of a popular entertainment: 'His formula for production is to hire top-notch stars and composers, set them off in a gilt-edged production, keep the comedy loud and lewd. By this formula Mr —'s shows are now grossing over $90,000 a week.' That is American; but this description applies to other besides American shows. To what degradation has a society fallen, which not only has such amusements but speaks of them without a sense of shame; among whose characteristic phrase-coinages are 'strip-tease' and 'sex appeal'! How strange that such things should appear, without any sense of incongruity, in a high-class paper! That is what I mean by saying that this generation might be called 'The Age without Standards'.

The life without standards exists in all epochs, but it is the peculiar danger of a rich society at whose feet every kind of facility, distraction and pleasure are poured in indiscriminate profusion. Commercialism helps the chaos. For the aim of commerce is not to sell what is best for people or even what they really need, but simply to sell: its final standard is successful sale. Such a society breeds the type which Plato calls the 'democratic' man, behind the lineaments of whose portrait, drawn more than 2000 years ago, we discern a contemporary face:

> He spends as much time and pains and money on his superfluous pleasures as on the necessary ones.... He sets all his pleasures on a footing of equality, denying to none equal rights and maintenance, and allowing each in turn, as it presents itself, to succeed to the government of his soul until it is satisfied. When he is told that some pleasures should be pursued and valued as arising from desires of a higher order, others chastised and enslaved because the desires are base, he will shut the gates of the citadel against the messengers of truth, shaking his head and declaring that one appetite is as good as another and all must have equal rights. So he spends his days indulging the pleasure of the moment, now intoxicated with wine and music, and then taking to a spare diet and drinking nothing but water; one day in hard training, the next doing nothing at all, the third apparently immersed in study. Every now and then he takes a part in politics, and jumps to his feet to say or do whatever comes into his head. Or he will set out to rival someone whom he admires, a soldier perhaps, or, if the fancy takes him, a man of business.*

Such a character is not wholly bad. It has moment of energy and intermittent spurts of goodness, but the desire or ambition of the moment masters it—now sex, now money, now something else, and it makes no distinction between good and bad, because it has no standards, no principle to rule and discipline it. 'Such a man's life', as Plato says, 'is subject to no order or restraint, and he has no wish to change an existence which he calls pleasant, free and happy.' But of all lives the life without standards is the most ignoble and barren, sweet in the mouth but bitter in the belly.

In this portrait of a fourth-century Athenian we see a phenomenon of our own age, the same indiscriminate mixture of good and bad, everything by turns and nothing long; as if the world was a department store, where men wandered from counter to counter, buying now goods of the highest quality and now mere junk. That is our peace-time world; not a civilisation but the raw material of one, something wholly inadequate either to the resources at our command or to the capacities of human nature, a moral anarchy waiting for some overruling ideal to discipline and order it. Without such an ideal we play a game of blind man's buff, where the blind player, plucked this way and that, turns irresolutely first in one direction, then in another and catches nobody. That weakness extends from life at home to policy abroad. Here, the autocracies have had the quick decision and concentrated energy which spring from a clearly seen ideal and are impossible without it. What have been the marks of England and America in their pre-war years? Slowness to move, wavering purpose, uncertainty of aim, 'safety first'. The initiative has been with others, and we have waited till they forced us to decide and act. In the struggle between Germany and the democratic countries 'something whole-hearted has faced the half-hearted' and our weakness has imperilled and still imperils not only the things we hold dearest but the future of the world. Democracy has not commanded the spiritual forces necessary for its task or even for its safety. It is not our fortune, or democracy, or even its political leaders that are to blame. The fault lies far deeper: it

> is not in our stars
> But in ourselves, that we are underlings.

'To will anything thoroughly', says a modern writer, 'demands asceticism, that is life-long devotion to a single ideal carefully selected.... Will always conquers culture, when it is mere culture and not Christianity which brings concentration, determination, energy and supernatural reinforcement.' The Germans have had the single ideal, the asceticism, the will; we have had culture without Christianity; or—for that is too hard a judgment—our will and our religion have been impaired, overlaid and confused. For the moment war has disciplined us, imposing standards and forcibly cutting out of life things which in peace-time disgraced it, compelling us to understand the saying 'Strait is the gate and narrow is the way which leads to life'. We have accepted perforce the narrowing of our way, and so far are nearer to the road to life. The country is united for a great purpose, in which no doubt our interests are involved but which far transcends them, and for which practically every member of the nation is ready to sacrifice pleasure, comfort, ease and life—many have sacrificed all. If that spirit lasted after the war, what an England, what a world we might have! But will it last when the urgency passes and the road broadens and we can walk where and as we will?*

There we have the major task of this generation; how to find a principle to rule life, and firm footing in the turbid flux of modern civilisation with its films, its motor cars, its advertisements, its commercialism, its showy and seductive abundance of all that the childish, acquisitive heart of man desires.

To be successful, we must realise that we are in the midst of two revolutions: a social and economic and political revolution; but also a spiritual revolution—the weakening or dissolution of the traditions and beliefs which for many centuries have ruled

Western civilisation and held it together. This revolution has been partly assisted and partly concealed from us by other shocks and revolutions which pressed more insistently on the attention; by the war; by class conflict and social change; by science transforming the economic system, disclosing possibilities which outrun imagination, and suggesting a new, materialist interpretation of life (which, however, is as old as the fourth century B.C.).

Throughout the nineteenth century, England had, so far as any country ever had such a thing, a definite philosophy of life, to which Christianity contributed most, but which was reinforced, to a far greater degree than is generally realised, by the clear and noble ideals of Hellenism, through the classical education received by the governing classes. It would be difficult to find any leaders of the age whose outlook on life was uninfluenced, if not formed, by one of these. In some, like Shaftesbury and Bright, Christianity was dominant; in others, like Mill and Morley, Hellenism; in Gladstone, Newman and Jowett the two streams met. But Christian ideals deeply influenced even those like Carlyle, George Eliot, Matthew Arnold and many others, who rejected Christianity. Indeed it was impossible to escape the influence of beliefs which filled the atmosphere and in which almost everyone was brought up. No country is ever permeated through and through by its religion; human nature is too varied, frail and rebellious, and its spiritual dress, even if it purports to be of single material, is more or less stained and patched. The nineteenth century, like all ages, was polytheistic, but it had a less mixed crowd of deities than the twentieth, transferred its allegiance far less lightly, and as a whole it acknowledged, even where it did not profess, a great religion. The nation as a whole had a philosophy of life which might be called Christian; it had a common belief and common standard of conduct; and at the lowest it was governed by the ideal of respectability, the indispensable virtue of our fathers. The nineteenth century had a soul, a spirit: what soul, what spirit, has ours? The child of the Victorian age was born into a world of stable traditions and clear standards and was shaped from birth in their strong moulds. The child of to-day is born into a world whose traditions and standards are weakened, a world with inherited good habits, but no ruling philosophy of life. Through the last and still more the present century, the solid and impressive mansion which had been slowly built up through centuries of Christian belief, was steadily bombed.*

Who dropped the bombs? Some would say, Science. But it would be more accurate to attribute the damage to the spirit of criticism which was at work long before, but in the twentieth century gathered momentum and threw off restraint. My own university education fell at the turn of the century and there is a strong contrast between the books read by my generation and by its successors. In my shelves, rows of books by Carlyle, Ruskin, Matthew Arnold, George Meredith, John Morley, Pater, Stevenson, Froude, date from my undergraduate days and indicate some of the influences, which, outside our ordinary studies, presumably formed my mind, and, I think, the minds of most of my contemporaries. Few of the present generation knows much more than the names of any of them except perhaps Matthew Arnold and Stevenson, and, when I was a young tutor, they had already been replaced by Shaw, Wells, Arnold Bennett and Galsworthy, to whom, after the last war, was added Aldous Huxley, a profounder and more acute mind than any of them. I do not say that Carlyle and Ruskin were major prophets, but they were prophets. That word could not be applied to Shaw, or Aldous Huxley, or Galsworthy. For prophets have two marks. They must be critics; all the Victorian writers were that; Arnold or Ruskin were as critical of their age as any modern. But the positive element must outweigh the critical. Prophets criticise because they wish to reconstruct; the positive element in them far outweighs the negative; cynicism and flippancy are words they do not know; a vision of better things dominates their mind and drives them on; their denunciations spring from an intense faith; and behind the evils which they wish to destroy rises the vision of a new heaven and a new earth, the new Jerusalem descending from God out of heaven. None of these things can be said of the great sophists of the last forty years, men of lively minds, keen interest in ideas, and with the gift of expression, who were read by the large educated public. They are essentially critics who have destroyed with great success but have constructed nothing; not even H. G. Wells, a man of constructive instincts, and eighteenth-century encyclopaedist, born out of due season.

Another contrast between the great Victorians and their successors is revealed in some words of George Meredith: 'I strive by study of humanity to represent it; not its morbid action. I have a tendency to do that, which I repress; for, in delineating it, there is no gain....Much of my strength lies in painting morbid emotion and exceptional positions, but my conscience will not let me so waste my time...My love is for epical subjects, not for cobwebs in a putrid corner; though I know the fascination of unravelling them.' The same sense of values to be preserved, of conscience in choice and treatment of a subject, appears in Kipling's *The Rabbi's Song* and in Thomas Hardy's *He resolves to say no more*. There is little trace of it in many writers of a later time, the Age without Standards, who have followed a precisely opposite principle.*

A generation educated under these influences bears their mark, and is better trained for destroying an old world than for building a new one. There is no virtue in being uncritical; nor is it a habit to which the young are given. But criticism is only the burying beetle that gets rid of what is dead, and, since the world lives by creative and constructive forces, and not by negation and destruction, it is better to grow up in the company of prophets than of critics. There is a sonnet by Robert Bridges which has no title, but of which the real subject is education:

Who builds a ship must first lay down the keel
Of Health whereto the ribs of Mirth are wed:
And knit, with beams and knees of Strength, a bed
For decks of Purity, her floor and ceil.

Upon her masts, Adventure, Pride and Zeal,
To fortune's wind the sails of Purpose spread:
And at the prow make figured Maidenhead
O'erride the seas and answer to the wheel.

And let him deep in memory's hold have stor'd
Water of Helicon: and let him fit
The needle that doth true with heaven accord:
Then bid her crew, Love, Diligence and Wit
With Justice, Courage, Temperance come aboard,
And at her helm the master Reason sit.

Such vessels are not built in the shipyard of Messrs Shaw, Lytton Strachey, Aldous Huxley & Co.*

The twentieth century was an age of demolition, in which only two forces were constructive. Commerce and Industry built up their great undertakings, as solid-seeming as the vast buildings which house them, and, like these, things of a day: Science laboured steadily at a more enduring creation: her palaces, firmly based, rise with steady growth to ever newer heights, and, like the giants of legend, her workers 'pile Ossa on Olympus and Pelion on Ossa, that men may climb to heaven':

> Ὄσσαν ἐπ' Οὐλύμπῳ μέμασαν θέμεν, αὐτὰρ ἐπ' Ὄσσῃ
> Πήλιον εἰνοσίφυλλον ἵν' οὐρανὸς ἄμβατος εἴη.

A magnificent and enduring work, and if science alone could save the world, her integrity, devotion and industry would save it. But pass from her kingdom to that of morals and religion, and you are in a waste land of shaken beliefs and shattered standards, where the house-breakers are still busy. Here the work of the twentieth century has been to destroy the settled convictions of the Victorian Age, and before their attack a solid, comfortable and in most ways noble view of life has crumbled.

No doubt some destructive work was inevitable. So long as

there is life in the world, each generation will react against its predecessor, correct it, go beyond it. The house that accommodates the fathers never quite suits the children. But house-breakers rarely remember that the human race lives most happily in houses which each generation modifies to suit its own needs, keeping what is serviceable in the old building, and incorporating it in the new; certainly it cannot live on a bare site covered by untidy rubbish and relics of what has been overthrown. There is a parable in the New Testament, of a man from whom an unclean spirit was cast out, and who went through dry places seeking rest, but finding none took to himself seven other evil spirits worse than himself; and the last state of that man was worse than the first. That parable might have been written for us. The Victorian age had its standards, its ends. The critics drove out its spirits—evil and good indiscriminately—and left the house empty, swept and garnished. Nature abhors a spiritual vacuum, and strange spirits occupied the vacant rooms—Nazism, Communism, Fascism, Pacifism—each demanding an exclusive worship, while those to whom these religions do not appeal, are apt, like 'the democratic man', to admit a succession of guests, some of them disreputable.*

So we stand to-day. There are items on both sides of the balance-sheet. On the debit side, there is the loss of standards, the loss of a definite philosophy of life, and the consequent loss of clear direction and steady drive. But there is a credit side too. Demolition was needed and the age of criticism has swept away some things which had to go and some which we are better without. We are less narrow, less prejudiced, more tolerant and humane than the weaker Victorians; we can apply to ourselves, as they could not, the words which Pericles uses of Athens and say: 'We give free play to all in our public life and carry the same spirit in our daily relations with each other; we have no black looks or angry words for our neighbour if he enjoys himself in his own way.' Perhaps we have less cant, hypocrisy and vulgarity, though these spirits usually manage, unobserved, to find new reincarnations in each age. Our vitality is undiminished; this is not a worn-out world, and its vigour is not seen only in science and industry; it has created two new 'religions'—in Russia and Germany—since the last war. Finally, we have a large fund of inherited virtues. There is an enormous amount of goodness and goodwill and right feeling and action in the modern world. Take, as a single example, a virtue so common in this country that we hardly notice it, the unselfish public spirit which shows itself in unpaid public service and in money given or bequeathed for public purposes. When a real storm comes and we know ourselves in danger, we still have the ancient virtues of England at call: witness heroism by land, sea and air; in bombed cities, courage and cheerfulness and endurance, self-help and help of others; the traditional kindliness and decency of the ordinary English folk. These are great assets, not to be forgotten.*

But in our satisfaction with our merits it is well to remember other less admirable sides of English life, of some of which I have spoken, and to reflect that we are living on character formed in the past by beliefs which are now shaken or destroyed. Character takes long to form, but it is not quickly destroyed. Lord Bryce was once asked: 'What do you think would be the effect of the disappearance of religious education from the schools?' 'I can't answer that', he replied, 'till three generations have passed.' We have inherited good habits, and habits persist almost indefinitely if there is nothing to destroy them. A plant may continue in apparent health for some time after its roots have been cut, yet its days are numbered. The case of Germany witnesses to the truth of this contention. Who, thirty years ago, would have believed a prophet who said that a decent, friendly, highly educated and civilised people, among whom Christianity was apparently still strong, would be capable of the persecution of the Jews, the horrors of the concentration camps, the barbarism, knowing neither justice nor mercy nor truth, shown in so many lands? How astonishing, we say, that such things could happen in the twentieth century! It is not in the least astonishing. The spiritual roots of Germany had been cut, and rootless virtues are precarious. But how strong are the roots of *our* virtues? The philosophy of life, the standards by which the Victorian and earlier ages were governed, have broken down. We are left with traditions and habits of conduct inherited from them, as the earth may for a time still receive light from an extinct star. But that light will not continue to shine, nor can these habits and traditions long survive the beliefs from which they grew. Those who reject Christian beliefs, cannot count on keeping Christian morals.*

Some prophetic words of Plato, which might have been written for this age, indicate our problem. 'It is not', he says, 'the life of knowledge, not even if it included all the sciences, that creates happiness and well-being, but a single branch of knowledge—the science of good and evil. If you exclude this from the other branches, medicine will be equally able to give us health, and shoemaking shoes and weaving clothes. Seamanship will still save life at sea and strategy win battles. But without the knowledge of good and evil, the use and excellence of these sciences will be found to have failed us.' Plato speaks the language of his own civilisation and talks of medicine, weaving, shoemaking and seamanship. To-day he would say that science, economics and sociology, industry and commerce will provide us with the frame of our society and satisfy its material needs, but that 'unless we have the knowledge of good and evil, their use and excellence will be found to have failed us'. It has been already 'found to have failed us'. Let us learn our lesson.†

This generation then has a double task: to create the new order, of which we are always speaking; or, more accurately, to guide the nation through one of the great social changes in its history; but also to train human beings fit to live in the new order, and, in Milton's words, 'to make in the towardly and pregnant soil of England a Nation of Prophets, of Sages and of Worthies'. New orders do not necessarily mean a great civilisation, nor do improved social conditions inevitably make better human beings. Inhabitants of a slum moved into a modern housing estate may carry their old habits with them and spoil their new surroundings; and we too may be unworthy tenants of an order however new and good. We have to transform a world with uncertain standards and vague values, with many virtues but no clear philosophy of life, into one which knows how to refuse evil and choose good, clear in its aims and therefore in its judgments and action. It will not be done merely by the extension of social services or the abolition of unemployment, important as these are, but by a change of mind and heart. That will not come of itself nor can it be left to chance. We must do what, in their different ways, Russia, Germany and Italy have done already; they have made great political and social changes, but they have not been content with these; they have trained men with a new outlook and a new way of life, conscious of an ideal which makes sacrifices pleasant and difficulties only a challenge to further effort. They have been concerned, after their fashion, with what Plato calls the science of good and evil, though their idea of good and evil may be very far from the true one. We have not: but unless we get a clear and right idea of good and evil, our new order will come to little, if it comes into being at all. It is a task for education in the widest sense, and needs first an educational system which will make it possible and next, within that system, an education which will achieve it.

CHAPTER II

CHARACTER AND ITS TRAINING

STANDARDS; a philosophy of life; a principle by which to judge and rule it; a formula or formulas to integrate our civilisation, our new order; some knowledge of the 'science of good and evil'. How are these to be given? They are being given every moment—in cinemas, in advertisements, in newspapers and books and parliament and pulpit, through everything that we see, hear and read; and much of it is disintegration rather than integration. It is the more important that the greatest of all formative forces, education, should make its voice heard decisively above the babel of confused crying.

But are its accents clear and does it do what we need? It may do nothing, or do exactly the opposite and only add to our confusion. Listen to a description of modern education and its effects by the well-known American thinker, Mr Walter Lippmann:

> There is an enormous vacuum where until a few decades ago there was the substance of education. And with what is that vacuum filled: it is filled with the elective, eclectic, the specialised, the accidental and incidental improvisations and spontaneous curiosities of teachers and student. There is no common faith, no common body of principle, no common moral and intellectual discipline. Yet the graduates of these modern schools are expected to form a civilised community. They are expected to govern themselves. They are expected to have a social conscience. They are expected to arrive by discussion at common purposes. When one realises that they have no common culture, is it astounding that they have no common purpose? That they worship false gods? That only in war do they unite? That in the fierce struggle for existence they are tearing Western society to pieces?...We have established a system of

education in which we insist that while everyone must be educated, yet there is nothing in particular that an educated man should know.*

Mr Lippmann argues that American education creates 'no common culture, no common faith, no common body of principle, no common moral and intellectual discipline', and that it fails to do so because it is a congeries of subjects which are excellent in themselves but have no common purpose or have forgotten what it was. British education is less elective and eclectic, but much of this criticism seems to be true of it, its results and its present tendencies.

Our education has great virtues. It is fully conscious of part of its duty and performs that part as well as can be expected of any human institution. It imparts the knowledge generally considered desirable. It produces the specialists which a complicated society needs to maintain its machine. It teaches its pupils to use their intellects. Doubtless, it might do all these things better, but it makes good provision for them. We should be admirably educated if we had to be nothing but technical or professional machines, carrying out the routine of government, industry, commerce and other functions necessary to a material civilisation. Unfortunately, we have also to be human beings. We are concerned not only with livelihood but with the good life. And of this our education is only partly aware. Here and there it trains men for it, uncertainly, sporadically, fitfully; and the training depends on the insight of individual teachers and the almost accidental existence of certain schools.

This defect in education is reflected and illustrated in the state of Europe, whose industry, commerce, science, technology, medicine, are first-rate. It is a superb building, admirably equipped with the latest material improvements. Materially, it speaks a common language. Its learned men, its technologists, its soldiers and sailors, its doctors and teachers, its lawyers and administrators, use the same tongue, understand each other, are able and ready to co-operate in their various vocations. We are advanced, united, international, in our material civilisation; when we pass beyond it, Babel begins—in our relations with others and even within ourselves. We and our education have been too absorbed in the matter of life to think of its spirit. We must restore to it a vitamin, deficient both there and in our life—a religion, a philosophy of living, a definite ideal to guide, discipline and dominate the lives of individuals and, through them, national life. Education, that maid-of-all-work, has to set her hand to as many duties as a general servant. But two things she should give everybody before her work is complete—an intellectual attitude to life and a philosophy of life. I would define the right intellectual attitude as threefold: to find the world and life intensely interesting; to wish to see them as they are; to feel that truth, in Plato's words, is both permanent and beautiful. And a philosophy of life? The right intellectual attitude to life is already a partial philosophy of it. It is complete, if you extend it to cover Goodness, Truth and Beauty, and define Goodness to cover those words which have been trumpet-calls to many generations, and, once sounded by unknown men far back in history, have been borne round the world on the waves of the spiritual air, now loud, now low, but never wholly silent: love, justice, courage, self-mastery, mercy, liberty. Philosophy passes into religion when these are seen to point to and derive their validity from that ultimate spiritual reality which we call God. Philosophy and an intellectual attitude are high-sounding terms; yet their rudiments are within the powers of any school-child—to find work interesting, to see the difference between fact and fiction, and to acquire an outlook, a habit of mind, a sense of values, an insight into 'the science of good and evil', which will later ripen into a rational conviction. The fundamental task of education is to put into the mind some idea of what these things are, some desire to pursue them. An education that does this is a success: an education that does less is a failure. Our education seems to me to do it only partially and sporadically.

Consider the School Certificate—and the majority of

children in secondary schools get no further—and ask what principle lies behind it, and you will probably conclude that if any principle integrates it, if any tie holds together its collection of loose sticks, it is an attempt to train some of the faculties and impart some of the knowledge which 'an educated person should possess'. Excellent so far; but this is not enough to produce 'a common faith, common culture, common body of principle'. From time to time reformers get busy. But they are more concerned with what the pupil must know and how his faculties should be trained, than with his sense of values and his knowledge of good and evil. And what he should know is interpreted in a utilitarian sense. Materialism continually besets education. Forty years ago it took a coarse form in the demand from a certain type of business man that secondary education should consist largely of book-keeping, typing, shorthand, and modern languages for commercial subjects. To-day our utilitarianism is more refined. All will be well, we are told, if we have more science, or more economics and sociology. And why not some American history, of which most of us are sadly ignorant? And now we are friends of Russia, more attention should be paid to Russian. And, when one comes to think of it, are we well prepared to deal with politics, knowing so little of other important countries, China, Japan, Latin America, and many, many others? Our ignorance of these things and much else is a grave handicap to living intelligently in a complicated world. But the remedy is not to crowd these subjects into an already overloaded school curriculum, or teach them to children, few of whom are interested in them, and none have the maturity of mind to grasp them properly. They are subjects for the adult, whose mind is mature and to whom they are practical and urgent problems, and there is no greater need than to give opportunities for their study through adult education. But that is not our method. Some country—let us call it Ruritania—rises above the political horizon, fills the newspapers and the public eye, becomes interesting and important for the moment. There is a general feeling that we do not know enough of Ruritania, and that something ought to be done about it. A public-spirited person, or an expert on Ruritania, writes to *The Times*. Teachers of Ruritanian point out how neglected the subject is in our schools and how few chairs of the Ruritanian language there are in the Universities, and urge that it should be included in the Higher Certificate syllabus and in language courses for a degree. The Board of Education is approached and blesses the project in guarded words. We all know this phenomenon: it occurs at least once a year. Generally—such is the force of human inertia and so many are the competing subjects—nothing is done. Ruritania passes out of the news and the agitation subsides into a few faint flickers at educational conferences. And that perhaps is fortunate. Otherwise another addition is made to an overcrowded curriculum, its chaos grows still more chaotic, still more devoid of system or plan; the shop-window is elaborately dressed but bears little relation to the goods in the shop; the face value of the currency is imposing, its purchasing power small. Such methods take us somewhere, but not where we need to go.*

Our utilitarianism reveals itself in the discussion of the modern languages to be taught in schools—shall French, German, Russian, Spanish, Italian, have the first place? Various arguments are brought forward, difficulty, intellectual discipline, commercial value, help to international understanding, available texts and other relevant points. But one most important consideration is hardly ever mentioned—the quality of the literature in the languages concerned. And yet a major criterion in the choice of a language is the wisdom and greatness to which its knowledge opens the door, and obviously languages differ greatly in this respect; the little attention that we pay to it betrays our habit of mind. Here perhaps I may be allowed a personal memory. I was taught French and German at school: in French we read books of the quality of *Tartarin de Tarascon, Le Capitaine Pamphile, Le Roi des Montagnes and Monte Cristo*; in German after two terms on *Easy Passages for German*

Translation we were thrown headlong into *Faust*, followed by Heine, Schiller and Lessing. Pedagogically, our German teacher's method was indefensible, educationally (in the highest sense of the word) it was right, that in a literature which has so little above the second rank we should have met its best writers and its one great genius. We learnt German, but also something more. Education would be the better if it had more of that spirit, and looked more steadily beyond material and immediate needs. Science, technology, economics, modern languages for commerce, are of course essential to the modern world. But their concern is with the means of life, not with its ends; and a clear view of ends is as essential to successful living as a mastery of means. We live—all of us—in two worlds; in the everyday world which changes in each age with the progress of material civilisation; and (whether we give it that name or not) in a spiritual world, without which Science could not believe in Truth, or Religion in God, or Good itself have any meaning. This is the world of values. To sacrifice it to science or economics or sociology or anything else is as fatal as to omit vitamins from the human diet. We do not pay enough attention to it.*

I have suggested that our secondary education, while as efficient in its actual teaching as any human institution is likely to be, suffers in general from lack of integration, from the absence of a spirit to order and guide its processes, and that in the choice and teaching of subjects it thinks more of what its pupils should know than of their outlook on life. What of proposals for its integration? There are many, and should soon be well if abundance of prescriptions were enough. Among them are education for freedom, for creativeness, for personality, for equality, for social change, for a dynamic society, for a world of science and technology. Dynamic, creative, personality, equality, liberty, democracy, science, social change—these comforting words are often flung about, without any exact idea of what they mean or how far they take us. We ought indeed to be free, dynamic and creative, to develop our personalities; we live in a world of social change and science and should know how to do it. But do any of these proposals take us far? Will they solve, do they show any awareness of, our deepest problem? Are they more than skating on a surface below which are unplumbed and unregarded depths? Education for freedom: the value of freedom depends on how it is used. For creativeness. To create what? For personality. To develop what kind of person? For equality or an equalitarian life. Lived at what spiritual level? For the 'highly technicalised twentieth-century civilisation'. To understand techniques will not teach us to use them for good purposes. For social change. What is the soul of the new world to be? For a dynamic society. Dynamic for what ends? The Gadarene swine were very dynamic; so is Germany. We must go deeper than any of these prescriptions will take us. Excellent as they are within their limits, they will not reach our real disease. The prescribers have never asked what should be the guiding principle of the State, whose citizens they have to train; and, deeper still, what the individual is to be or to seek to be; they have never defined the good life for man. It is not enough to give people the knowledge necessary to live in a 'highly technicalised civilisation' or even the power of thinking clearly, unless they are given a clear conception of the kind of pattern they should weave, of the life which they and their fellow-citizens should lead. Without this they may be equipped with the means to realise their end, but they will be in the dark or in twilight about the end itself. Knowledge of science and technology and economics is not the end; nor are creativeness or freedom or even truth; they are indispensable to civilisation but too narrow a basis for it, and schemes that look no further leave us where we are—able to make and do almost all we want, but uncertain what we wish to make or do or be, ignorant of the fundamental 'science of good and evil'.*

Anyone who looks at the present state of the world must feel that this is the problem of which we need to think most. But we shy away from it, partly through short-sightedness, partly through moral and intellectual cowardice. It is at any time the most difficult and dangerous of all problems, and doubly so to-day when the beliefs of Western civilisation are shaken. We know what to believe about science and modern languages and economics, or at any rate think that we can find out, or at worst that it does not so much matter if we make mistakes about them. So we succumb to the common and disastrous human instinct to run away from difficult decisions, and concentrate on freedom or creativeness or equality or technology, as if these, however important, were substitutes for something more fundamental. But the decision must be made: our own character and the character of our society depend on it: if we decide wrongly they will be bad, if we decide right they will be good; if we hesitate and haver, they will be impotent and at the mercy of any strong force.

But, it will be said, some of our education at least is 'integrated', and integrated round the very principle for which you are arguing, round standards and a definite view of life. Are we not always talking about character? Have we not always believed that it is more important than brains? Has not its development been the chief aim of English education, since Arnold defined his ideal as the training of Christian gentlemen? 'Christian', 'gentlemen'—what do these words connote except character and a philosophy of life built on this? And have we not been, in large measure, successful? Onlookers have a clearer view of the game than the players; and the feature which foreigners admire in English residential schools, and find wanting in their own, is the power of training character. Is not this the principle of integration which we want, and could there be a better?

I hesitate to introduce into my argument an institution which excites lively passions; there is more objectivity in a bull looking at scarlet than in some critics contemplating residential schools. Yet it is the fact that the three most original British achievements in education are (in chronological order) the Residential School, the Workers' Educational Association and the Scout and Guide Movement. Other countries may equal or surpass our elementary, secondary, technical and university education; but these three products are creations of our own and are all known, admired and imitated abroad. Among these the residential school aims at producing, and on the whole does successfully produce, a definite type of human being with clear standards, and achieves more nearly what I have been pleading for than any other of our educational institutions. There are other schools which send their pupils out into the world with a definite attitude to life, but it is especially characteristic of the residential school to do it. Whether it likes it or not, it cannot help producing a common attitude to life among its pupils, not in virtue of its curriculum, which does not differ from that of the day school, but because it is residential. It has its pupils' whole time and their whole life, their hours of leisure as well as of work, for eight months of the year. In such circumstances a common ethos (which may leave room for great individual differences) must develop automatically. The residential school cannot in its own interests neglect the character-training of its inmates or leave it wholly to the home. Nor can it neglect religion, at least in a country which sets store by religion. Hence the school chapel and religious worship and teaching and the development of a view of life. And, at its best, the residential school has been and is admirably successful in producing men with right values and a clear view of life.*

But it has not always been at its best, and then it has both succeeded and failed; succeeded in training certain moral qualities, and failed because our definition of character has been too narrow. Character means for us courage, truthfulness, trustworthiness, a sense of honour, independence, fair play, public spirit and leadership. These are national ideals and on the whole national virtues, and in developing them the English race and the English school compare favourably with any other. They are the qualities necessary if men wish to live together in a society, and the English insistence on them partly explains why we have so far been able to work passably well the most difficult form of society, democracy, in which there is a minimum of compulsion and a maximum of free co-operation. But these by themselves do not complete character. If a man has them, he should be able to 'withstand in the evil day, and having done all, to stand'. But life is wider and richer than the traditional virtues of the residential school. It includes art and thought and science, and all the capacities which create these and all the activities which they cover. Further, life is dynamic as well as static; it involves motion as well as standing and withstanding; and motion, if it is to be of any purpose, is towards a goal, rightly chosen and clearly seen. It is not enough to be able to do right, unless we know the right; and this knowledge is part of character. Here we are less successful. Indeed the history of mankind might be described by a cynic as a series of splendid expeditions towards the wrong goal or towards no goal at all, led by men who have all the gifts of leadership except a sense of direction, and every endowment for achieving their ends except the knowledge of ends worth achieving. We must not forget in our education this element, a sense of direction. We do forget it, if we are content that our schools should merely impart knowledge, develop and discipline the intelligence, train character in the narrow sense. They must also be places where the mind is enriched by the right visions and where the ends of life are learned.*

The English find it difficult to take these aspects of school seriously. There is a common assumption among them that a boy good at games will be good in practical life, and that a boy good at books will not. Neither of these beliefs is borne out by facts or shared by any other nations except those of English blood. But Englishmen nurture in the depth of their hearts a feeling that intellectual interests are enervating. They do not really believe that the claim of Pericles for Athens—'Our intellectual interests involve no effeminacy'—could be true about anybody. They are better pleased with the ideal of the Spartans 'who from their cradle cultivate manliness by laborious discipline'. The long roll of English statemen and men of action from Raleigh and Chatham to Gladstone and Cromer, who have found inspiration, delight and consolation in literature, is nothing to them. they would have thought Wolfe incapable of taking Quebec if they had known his enthusiasm for Gray's *Elegy*, and been nervous about Charles James Fox's passion for Euripides, if his gambling debts had not suggested that he was a man of affairs. They would regard Napoleon's and Wellington's fondness for the *De Bello Gallico* as a dangerous symptom; as doubtless they would have disbelieved in Caesar's practical capacity, because he wrote a book on the theory of grammar during his Gallic campaigns, and quoted Menander when he crossed the Rubicon.*

Hence the theory which is often heard at prize-days. Some distinguished general or admiral, some successful business man, returns for a few hours to the haunts of his youth and expounds his sentiments on the principles of education. They may be read in *The Times* any June or July, when English schools normally hold their prize-days. The speaker points out that it is not always the successful schoolboy who succeeds in after life. He himself was no good at work and never much cared for it; but then, he reminds his audience, it is not learning Latin and Greek that one looks for at school, but training of character and learning to play the game. How well one knows this doctrine! In any case it is superfluous. To preach it to schoolboys is carrying coals to Newcastle. Few of them need to be warned against over-valuing Latin and Greek, against a too arduous devotion to intellectual interests. But there is a graver objection to it. The doctrine is false. A character, trained in this limited sense, is admirable within its limits but inadequate to the needs of the modern world. It is deficient *as a character*. It may have, and at its best undoubtedly has, powers of leadership. But it is the leadership of a corporal or a sergeant. Such an education produces a superb army of N.C.O.'s; whereas the real business of the school is to train staff-officers, men able to face unexpected emergencies, to lead an army and not merely a platoon, to plan a campaign.

It would of course be grossly unfair to suppose that the residential school has always produced such limited types or produced nothing else. It was very different in Arnold's hands: he broadened the basis of education; whatever he taught—classics, history or scripture—he taught in its relation to life; he trained character, but he gave a philosophy of life to support it. And in this he has had many successors. Anyone who doubts this and supposes that residential schools turn out nothing but a regimented type without intellectual or other interest can refute his error by glancing through the pages of *Who's Who* or examining the names in any Cabinet and asking whether its members who were educated at residential schools compare unfavourably with those who were not. Still this has been the besetting danger of the residential school and the sharpest weapon of their critics. At their weakest they have sent out boys furnished with invaluable qualities of character but with character trained on too narrow lines; they have thought it enough to give them 'a habit of good behaviour without an intellectual basis'—the phrase is Plato's, who points out how inadequate an equipment this is for life in a disordered world. In this they have reflected the weaknesses of the nation itself, its Philistinism, its reluctance to think things out or to base conduct on principle.*

What then shall we do?

Education is a vast continent and it will make for clearer thinking if we divide it into three main provinces, corresponding to the three main needs of human life. All men need to make a living—not a bare one, but the best that conditions allow. All men live in a society. All men have a personality to develop and the power of living ill or well. For all these education must provide, and it must therefore include a vocational element, a social or, as the Greeks would have called it, a political element, and a spiritual element. Men must learn to earn a living, to be good members of a society, to understand the meaning of the phrase 'the good life'; and education must help them to achieve these three ends. It must do this not for a limited class but for every citizen, though it will do it in different ways for different people.

The new society, then, like every society, will need three main kinds of education—vocational, social, spiritual. It must provide for its material existence and for the running of its machine, and the education dealing with this may be called vocational. It will need its technologists and skilled workers to feed it, clothe it and supply the necessities, comforts and even luxuries of life; its doctors, scientists, economists, teachers, administrators. So it will have every variety of technical education, and in its places of higher study it must provide not only for Medicine, Science and Applied Science, but for such subjects as Economics, Psychology, Sociology, Public and Colonial and Business Administration: the list can be completed by studying the Calendar of the London School of Economics. That, of course, is not to say that everyone will study all, or even any, of those subjects. In addition to training the numerous and various specialists which it requires, a society should give its educated members at least, not indeed specialist knowledge, but some perception of the general conditions and possibilities of modern civilisation, and a sense of the importance and uses of the techniques and specialisms essential to it.

Then our society will need social or political education, a training in citizenship, as we call it, which I leave to a later chapter, passing on to the third aspect of education—that which fits a man for living well. In practice it cannot be separated from the other two—education for a vocation and for citizenship—but in aim it differs from them. It has no name. You can call it the education of personality, but that word in turn needs definition, and it is simplest to take the old Greek analysis and think of it as the education of body, mind and character, to the highest degree of which each individual is capable. Of this immense subject I shall only touch on a side which, for want of a better word, may be called spiritual. The efficiency of a community will depend on its technical and vocational education, its cohesion and duration largely on its social or political education. But the quality of its civilisation depends on something else. It depends on its standards, its sense of values, its idea of what is first-rate and what is not. The vocational and the social aspects of education are essential, but the most fatal to omit is the spiritual aspect; fatal, because its absence may be long unperceived, and, as with an insidious disease, a State may suffer from it and be unconscious of its condition till the complaint has gone too far to cure. And this spiritual element is precisely what we tend to ignore. Yet nothing is more needed at the moment. The body of our civilisation risks destruction by war, and we are too distressed by that to notice that its soul is already more than half drowned in the turbid river of modern life.

During the last war the salvation of the world was assigned to science. Now we are disillusioned. Science, like medicine, is an integral part of civilised life. It is difficult for human beings to maintain health without doctors, but medicine is not health. It is difficult for a civilisation to be sound without science, but science is not civilisation, and few people can suppose that salvation is its business. To-day we tend to assign that rôle to psychology, economics and sociology. These branches of knowledge are indispensable to our civilisation. We have not enough of them. We need more. But though adjuncts and auxiliaries, they too are not saviours of society, and if we fix our hopes on them the year 1960 will find us so much further down the hill and looking for some other force to help us to recover our lost ground. Our knowlege of the sciences, natural or social, fixes the limits of the course within which the yachts on which humanity is embarked must sail, but does not indicate the goal of their voyage, still less supply wind to fill their sails.

The forces that move the world need to be informed and disciplined by the intellect, but they are not in themselves intellectual. Is there any great event in history which does not bear out that truth? Economic or social conditions may prepare the way; the moving force is a vision. The ardour that created modern Germany and modern Russia came from a vision, even if it was one seen through bloodshot eyes. An eternal trait of men is the need for vision and the readiness to follow it; and if men are not given the right vision, they will follow wandering fires. One tragedy of our world is that Hitler had a vision and his opponents had not. The weakness of England and of America is that (with plenty of science and a quantum at least of economics and sociology) they have seen no clear vision. Indistinct and blurred figures stir them in their uneasy sleep, but have not yet taken form. That has been a grave weakness in this war; it will be a much graver one, when we face the problems of peace.*

If we are to cure it, we must look beyond (without overlooking) science, technology, economics, sociology, handicrafts, subjects 'with a vocational bias', and recall and extend a statement by Professor Whitehead that would probably surprise most English people: 'Moral education', he says, 'is impossible without—' What? Residential schools, games, a happy and disciplined family life? No, none of these. 'Moral education is impossible without the habitual vision of greatness.' It could not be put more strongly—*'impossible', 'habitual* vision' (not a chance and occasional glimpse). Outside Plato, there is no profounder saying about education.†

A 'habitual vision of greatness' is necessary not only to moral education, but to all education. A teacher cannot give an adequate training in anything unless he knows, and can make his pupil see, what is great and first-rate in it. How can you train a surgeon unless you show him the finest technique of surgery; or a teacher, unless he knows the best methods of educational practice; or an architect, unless he is familiar with the great examples of his art? So, too, with all subjects from building to farming, from carpentry to Greek prose. Much else may enter the student's training; but there is no stimulus like seeing the best work in the subject which he studies; he will have no standards, no conception of the goal to which he painfully struggles, unless he sees the best; he will slip insensibly to lower levels of ideal and practice, unless it is continually before his mind, unless, in fact, he has the 'habitual vision of greatness' to attract, direct and inspire. In all studies and in all spheres of life, knowledge of the best is essential to success. And if this is necessary in medicine and teaching and architecture and town-planning, must it not be necessary in character? And is not Whitehead right when he says that you cannot train character 'without the habitual vision of greatness'? Mere character training in the narrow sense could be carried out by a drill-sergeant; courage, endurance, fair-play, discipline, could be learnt on a parade ground, and the work would need a far less highly qualified staff than those of a school. There is something more to character training than this. It is common and disastrous to forget that the character must be trained through the intellect as well as by other means, and that part of the work of education is to enrich the vision of its pupils and thereby train their characters. A school that fails to do this is failing to do its work. That is a truth of which teachers and pupils cannot too often remind themselves. What more important service can school or university do for their pupils than show them the best things that have been done, thought and written in the world, and fix these in their minds as a standard and test to guide them in life? Men's achievements depend not only on the qualities of character (in the narrow sense) with which they tackle their task but also on knowing what is first-rate; ill-success in every field of life is due quite as much to ignorance of what is good as to incapacity to achieve it. One is apt to think of moral failure as due to weakness of character: more often it is due to an inadequate ideal. We detect in others, and occasionally in ourselves, the want of courage, of industry, of persistence which leads to defeat. But we do not notice the more subtle and disastrous weakness, that our standards are wrong, that we have never learnt what is good.

Take an example. The nineteenth century built cities of incredible ugliness, the twentieth century spoils the beauty of the country with hideous bungalows and defaces the beauty of Oxford by making it an industrial town—in perfect innocence but with disastrous results. It was not malice aforethought, it was pure ignorance. It was the absence of a standard. It was the failure to know what was really good. How essential then that the citizen should know and desire the best things—the best things in art and architecture, the best things in literature and thought, the best things in politics, industry and commerce, the best professional ideals, the best things in human character! In the perfectly educated community at least the leaders, and so far as possible their public, would have seen this vision not only in their own immediate work, but in many fields. They would know the best in imperial, national and municipal politics; in town-planning, housing, and the social services; in the earning and spending of money; in social and family relations; in thought and art, intellect and individual life. The more fields and the clearer the vision, the richer and greater national life would be. School and university cannot do more than begin such a work; their pupils are too undeveloped, their time too short, to take in such a panorama. It must be begun at school, but it needs to be carried on and completed in later life and demands a provision for adult education which our shortsightedness has not yet dreamed of making. How inadequate is an education which fails to impart something of such visions! How misconceived is one which never makes the attempt! That is the disastrous flaw in the doctrine of those who suppose that a school has done its duty when it has taught pluck, self-reliance, truthfulness and the art of playing the game. These are indeed splendid qualities. But they are not enough to make a world. Achieve them and we shall still have achieved only a part of human virtue. The most indispensable viaticum for the journey of life is a store of adequate ideals, and these are acquired in a very simple way, by living with the best things in the world—the best pictures, the best buildings, the best social or political orders, the best human beings. The way to acquire a good taste in anything, from pictures to architecture, from literature to character, from wine to cigars, is always the same—be familiar with the best specimens of each.

Knowledge of the first-rate gives direction, purpose and drive: direction, because it shows what is good as well as what is bad; purpose, because it reveals an ideal to pursue; drive, because an ideal stirs to action. To have seen Oxford or Cambridge, Edinburgh or Bath makes a nineteenth-century industrial city and a drab or 'picturesque' suburb repulsive, or at least pricks the conscience and stirs a sense of something wrong. The sight of goodness in life or in literature or history gives a standard and a challenge. If anyone has been able to compare the first-rate with the second-rate, his criticism will not be merely bitter and barren, but creative, born of a vision perceiving the good, dominated by it and desiring to bring it to birth. 'The intelligence of every soul rejoices at beholding Reality, and once more gazing on Truth is replenished and made glad.'*

In the fable from which these words are quoted, Plato, describing how each human soul before birth drove across heaven in the company of gods, and saw Beauty, Justice, Courage and the other virtues, says that success in life depends on how far, among the shadows, confusions and distractions of earth, the soul retains the memory of that vision. Plato's story is a parable of a good education.

CHAPTER III

THE TRAINING OF CHARACTER THROUGH HISTORY AND LITERATURE

OUR education then should not be satisfied with imparting the information which a pupil requires, equipping him for a vocation, teaching him how to use his mind. It should send him out with a definite spiritual attitude to life, and the material and basis for a definite philosophy of living. It should have the aim which it would probably profess to-day, which it would certainly not disclaim, but which in general it pursues half-heartedly and ineffectually, and in the university stage, especially in the newer universities, wholly abandons—the aim which education had 2300 years ago. Here is a description of the training of a Greek boy in the fifth century B.C.; consider, as you read it, if it would apply to our English education.

Education begins in the first years of childhood. As soon as the child can understand what is said, nurse and mother and the father himself exert themselves to make the child as good as possible, at each word and action teaching and showing that this is right and that wrong, this honourable and that dishonourable, this allowed by God and that not allowed. At a later stage they send him to teachers and tell them to attend to his conduct far more than to his reading and writing. And the teachers do so, and when the boy has learned his letters, they put into his hands the works of great poets, and make him read and learn them by heart, sitting on his bench at school. These are full of instruction and of tales and praises of famous men of old, and the aim is that the boy may admire and imitate and be eager to become like them. The music teachers, in the same way, take care that their young pupil learns self-control, and does nothing wrong, and when they have taught him to play, they teach him the poems of good lyric poets, and set these to music and make their harmonies and rhythms familiar to the children's souls, in order that they may become gentler and more rhythmical and harmonious and so fitted for speech and action. For the life of man in every part needs rhythm and harmony. Then they send the boy to the teacher of gymnastic, in order that the perfect body may serve the virtuous mind, and that he may not be compelled by physical defects to play the coward in war or in the other activities of life.*

Note here the aim—the overwhelming insistence on producing a definite type of character, a definite attitude to life. Education is conceived as spiritual training, and all its subjects, whatever else they are, are also food of the soul. That should be our model. Note too the methods; this steeping of the pupil in what is first-rate in 'stories and praises of famous men', in order that he 'may imitate them and wish to become like them'; this discipline of the body, not for the body's sake but that the body may be 'the servant of the virtuous mind'. That is the education which all human beings in all ages need.

It may seem a great narrowing of education; nothing about information or mental discipline; no word of science or economics; a restriction of it to training in goodness, to loving what is right and hating what is wrong. It is no doubt an excessive simplification, an over-concentration on one element; but for this age the emphasis is in the right place, nor does it in any way exclude other elements; it only stresses the supreme importance of character-training. Such an ideal would not cause any upheaval in our education, or any serious recasting of the curriculum; it would only involve a change of attitude and emphasis in the teaching of certain subjects. Visions of greatness in human life and character are to our hand in two subjects taught in every school—literature and history, including the Bible, which is both literature and history.

Here then we shall find visions of the first-rate in human life and character. But to see them clearly, we must read literature and history in a particular way. There are many ways of reading both. Take history. Most of us treat it as a panorama, often broken and dim, in which are seen the adventures of man on the earth from earliest beginnings to the last syllable of recorded time. We read it vaguely, the mind caught by a dramatic scene, a striking character or event, an interesting fact: the kaleidoscope revolves, the combinations change, and, unless the memory is retentive, pattern and colours fade from the mind. Or, again, we read with purpose, focussing the mind on some special aspect; we concentrate perhaps on the discovery of particular facts, or the study of great movements, on the growth of civilisation or the rise and fall of peoples, on constitutional development or political thought, on nationalism or colonial expansion or social change. All these ways of studying are legitimate and necessary, but will not help us, except accidentally, in our present purpose. If we wish to find spiritual values and patterns of goodness in literature or history, we must look for them as deliberately as, if we were primarily interested in economics, we should note in our reading allusions to industry or trade or wages or anything that threw light on the working of economic forces. The study of history in schools changes. In my youth it is supposed to have stressed kings, generals and nobles, diplomacy and war; then it became fashionable to concentrate on social aspects and the life of the common people. It includes this and much more. But ultimately it is the story of the slow ascent of man from the animal to the savage, and from the savage to modern civilisation. In this story lie the deepest interest and most fruitful lessons, and here we can find what we are looking for. Many things have conditioned and contributed to the ascent of humanity; biology, climate, economics have played a part; but so have great men. Here we are on the track of the examples, the inspiration that we were seeking—on the track of the first-rate. It is on this side of history that we must concentrate if we are looking for standards and values and the first-rate in human nature and conduct. The record of peoples and civilisation and the growth and decline of institutions and nations offer no doubt visions of greatness; Greece was more than Pericles, Rome than Caesar, Britain than Cromwell or Chatham or Pitt.

But it is in the personalities of history that we see most clearly courage and persistence, desire for wisdom and devotion to good—the great positive forces of the world by which humanity has climbed from cave and forest into a clearer air. Montaigne has written the motto for such a study of history: 'I would have the teacher remember the goal of his labours and be more concerned to impress on his pupil the characters of Hannibal and of Scipio than the date of the fall of Carthage.'*

Here certain distinctions are necessary. The makers of civilisation fall into three main classes—men of action, men of thought and knowledge, men of vision—a class which includes religious thinkers and teachers, poets and artists. These three classes make the rope by which men, with many halts and slips, climb slowly into a clearer air; all contribute to its strength: and seen from outside the three strands are combined so closely that it is hard to tell what each contributes or where they interlace. Some people suffer from colour-blindness, and can see only one strand. Thus early Christian fathers, like Tertullian, could not see the strand of thought and knowledge: thus in modern times Mr Wells sees little else, and in it sees chiefly the threads of science. But it is important to realise that the rope is of triple ply, and, so far as possible, to disentangle its components; we shall not understand civilisation if we forget any of the strands; we shall misunderstand it, if we do not clearly distinguish their contribution. It is difficult to exaggerate the influence of Faraday, Darwin and Pasteur, or, in a narrower field and for a shorter time, of men like Adam Smith; but their influence is wholly different from the influence of Socrates and Plato and the Stoics, of Christ, of St Augustine and St Thomas, or again from that of Alexander, Augustus, Charlemagne, Cromwell, Napoleon. No truism could be more obvious, but how often it has been forgotten! Each of the strands in turn is apt to seem, to those interested in it, to be the whole rope. In every age the strongest force fills the common eye and distorts the common judgment. In the past, religion was the offender, and the Church disregarded science or took the function of science into its own hands, and at various times decided that the earth was flat, that the Antipodes did not exist, that Hell was in the centre of the earth, and that the Creation took place some 6000 years ago. When religion restricted itself to its own function, the turn of science came, and popular imagination and some scientists made for the characteristic force of the age claims equally extravagant, unjustified and fallacious, and assigned it a dictatorship over life. As previously religion, so now science, like Bottom in Shakespeare, is to absorb every part in the drama: 'An I may hide my face, let me play Thisby too.' To-day, we are disillusioned but hardly wiser; for the pre-eminence allotted to science is being transferred to politics. Germany and Italy have looked for salvation to dictators, and we tend to think that the world will be saved by sociology and economics, by a managed currency or the organisation of international trade, by 'new orders' and 'planning'. Thus:

> Opinion gilds, with varying rays,
> These painted clouds that beautify our days:
> Hope builds as fast as knowledge can destroy.

But the rope will not bear the weight of humanity if it has only one strand or even two. Science and politics are essential but they are not enough without the spiritual strand, which, using the word in the widest sense, we may call religion.*

Therefore, in reading history as the record of human progress, education must see all three strands in the rope—spiritual, intellectual, political—study the men in whom they are embodied, and do justice to all. In fifth-century Athens it must remember Socrates and Democritus as well as Pericles; in the twelfth century A.D., St Bernard and John of Salisbury as well as Henry I and Frederick Barbarossa; in the sixteenth, Sir Thomas More and Copernicus as well as Henry VIII and Luther; in the nineteenth, Darwin and Shaftesbury as well as Bismarck and Cavour. We must judge these men in the light not only of their own age, but of all time, and estimate their contribution to civilisation *sub specie aeternitatis*, trying to read the writing of the Recording Angel and to divine the sentence of the Last Judgment. Here Time helps, and looking back we can discern the qualities that have brought mankind on, and those which have kept them back; the men and the nations who have deserted the army and dropped out of the struggle, and those who have been victorious or by their faith and endurance have made victory possible for others. Contemporary judgments are often reversed:

> O'er that wide plain, now wrapt in gloom,
> Where many a splendour finds its tomb,
> Many spent fames and fallen mights—
> The one or two immortal lights
> Rise slowly up into the sky
> To shine there everlastingly.

In the ascent of humanity, slow, devious and broken, Socrates is seen to matter more to the world than Pericles, St Bernard than Frederick, Sir Thomas More than Henry VIII, Pasteur and Darwin and, perhaps, Shaftesbury than Bismarck. Indeed in our survey we run the risk of undervaluing the men of action. They are an essential strand in the rope; and possibly a statesman who combines greatness with goodness, even if he contributes less to civilisation, deserves no less credit for his work than a great religious teacher or social reformer, or man of science; for his task, if it is rightly done, is even more difficult than theirs.*

Having distinguished the three strands, political, scientific, spiritual, we can turn to look more closely at the great men, and learn what is first-rate in human nature by studying those who have embodied it. And here turning to what may be called the life of the spirit, we must again distinguish different types. There are men who have done in the spiritual world what Darwin and Pasteur did in the world of nature—revealed a new attitude and outlook, and so enabled mankind to live on levels which without their vision it could not have reached. These are the prophets and religious teachers, who with a few words make revolutions in the spiritual life of mankind; like the utterance of Hosea: 'I desire mercy and not sacrifice, and the knowledge of God more than burnt-offerings', or the words of Christ: 'Ye have heard that it hath been said, Thou shalt love thy neighbour and hate thine enemy. But I say unto you, Love your enemies, do good to them that hate you: that ye may be the children of your Father which is in heaven.' Such utterances change the world; higher levels of existence are revealed; a new life is conceived, even if it takes millennia to bring it to birth.*

Then there are men to whom we owe a different revelation—that of goodness in action. Such, in one aspect of his life, was Socrates; such was St Bernard of Clairvaux, than whom few men are better worth study in difficult times, for he lived in an iron age. In the world there was lawlessness and savagery, in the Church a corruption, to which our time, so critical of the 'failure of the Church', offers no parallel. It would have been natural if he had swum with the tide, or taken refuge from it in a hermitage or lapsed into pessimism and denunciation. Instead, patiently and resolutely, he threw himself into the desperate battle, turned the rout and made a better world possible. If there had not been many such men, saints canonised and uncanonised, famous and unknown, mankind would not have advanced:

> Their shoulders held the heavens suspended;
> They stood, and earth's foundations stay.

We can perhaps learn more from them than from the prophets, for their virtues are nearer to our capacities, if not to our needs.†

Now turn from history to literature, the other great treasury of the first-rate in human nature and life. Here again, it is a question of angle of approach. In a work of prose or poetry we may be interested in date, sources, the biography of the writer, the contemporary or historical interest of his work; or in its technical aspects, in construction, metre, language; or we may read it for pure pleasure, indifferent to any other consideration; or we may study it deliberately as a vision of the world and of life. It is of this angle of approach that I wish to speak, and I would define it more exactly by saying that literature is a study, combined with delight, in the art of living, a vision of what is first-rate in human nature and life.

Literature, as a revelation of the first-rate in human nature and life, may take the form of direct exposition. Thus Matthew Arnold's *Morality* is a contrast between the spontaneous, effortless forces of Nature, and Morality, struggling and laborious, yet with a divine quality which Nature does not possess: thus Wordsworth's *Ode to Duty* is a balancing, almost a discussion, of two forms of goodness, the free, natural goodness,

> When love is an unerring light
> And joy its own security,

and one controlled and fortified by the law of duty; thus *The Character of the Happy Warrior* is a plain enumeration of the qualities which seemed to Wordsworth the best armour for the battle of life. These poems—and much of *The Prelude*—read almost like passages from Plato or Spinoza or Kant, or some philosophical or religious writer. In them poetry becomes deliberate criticism of life, unsystematic moral philosophy, written by men of imaginative genius (who are sometimes as good introductions to the subject as the philosophers). Such poems, like philosophy, are usually better appreciated and more enjoyed after the age of twenty than before it.*

Then there are poems where the ideas are no longer abstract but clothed in a concrete form. In this class come works like Wordsworth's *Leech-Gatherer*, a story of a walk on a moor during which the poet met an old man gathering leeches in the ponds.

None of his poems better illustrates the poet's power which he so modestly describes:

In common things that round us lie
  Some random truths he can impart;
  The harvest of a quiet eye
  That broods and sleeps on his own heart;

in none has imaginative insight found more perfect poetic expression. It can be read almost without reference to the idea which it embodies and which the sub-title, '*Resolution and Independence*', records; but that idea dominated the poet's mind, even if a reader may not notice it.*

Then again there are poems, like *The Faery Queen, Paradise Lost, Prometheus Unbound, The Idylls of the King*, in which a view of life is present, but latent. In all of them it is easy to forget or disregard the philosophy they embody, and, when the moral or idea in them loses its interest, the story may survive by its own vitality: as *Paradise Lost* has outlived its theology without losing any of its greatness, and remains a masterpiece though it no longer justifies the ways of God to man.†

In all these types of poetry a view of life is present, submerged in each at different depths. In *The Happy Warrior* it stands out and strikes the mind at once; in *The Leech-Gatherer* it may escape notice; in *The Faery Queen* or *The Idylls of the King* it must be looked for, if it is to be seen. Spenser, for instance, can be read for many reasons and looked at from many angles. We may be interested in his poetic development,in his vocabulary and versification, or in the vicissitudes of his stormy life; or we can lose ourselves in a world of romance, where, as on tapestry, knights and ladies, magicians and fairies move against a background of seas and palaces and

Forests and enchantment drear
Where more is meant than meets the ear.

But it is equally legitimate, and for our present purpose important, to be aware of another side of *The Faery Queen*. This is what a nineteenth-century critic, who looked for the view of life in *The Faery Queen*, found there:

The unity is one of character and its ideal. That character of the completed man, raised above what is poor and low, and governed by noble temper and pure principles, has in Spenser two conspicuous elements. In the first place, it is based on manliness. It is not merely courage, it is not merely energy, it is not merely strength. It is the quality of soul which frankly accepts the conditions in human life, of labour, of obedience, of effort, of unequal success; whch does not quarrel with them or evade them, but takes for granted with unquestioning alacrity that man is called—by his call to high aims and destiny—to a continual struggle with difficulty, with pain, with evil, and makes it the point of honour not to be dismayed or wearied out by them. It is a cheerful and serious willingness for hard work and endurance, as being inevitable and very bearable necessities, together with even a pleasure in encountering trials which put a man on his mettle, an enjoyment of the contest and the risk, even in play. It is the quality which seizes on the paramount idea of duty, as something which leaves a man no choice; which despises and breaks through the inferior considerations and motives—trouble, uncertainty, doubt, curiosity—which hang about and impede duty; which is impatient with the idleness and childishness of a life of mere amusement, or mere looking on, of continued and self-satisfied levity, of vacillation, of clever and ingenious trifling.

All this is undoubtedly present in *The Faery Queen* and it is possible both to enjoy the poem as poetry, and see and saturate oneself in the ideal which Dean Church found in it. And it is worth finding.*

So far I have been speaking of poets, who had some moral in their minds and intended to convey a lesson. But the moralists are not necessarily the best moral teachers: the first-rate exists and is felt, even though no one calls attention to it. It is, as the Greek critic said of sublimity, an echo of greatness of mind, and when greatness is present, the waves of the air are stirred. The English are fortunate in having not only the greatest poet in the world, but one whose sense of good and evil is nearly unerring. Almost every type of character, and every interest of human beings, except religion and science, are to be found in Shakespeare. There is virtue and vice, greatness and pettiness, Claudius and Iachimo and Iago as well as Horatio and Imogen and Cordelia, Polonius and Osric as well as Kent and Paulina; but there is no doubt about the difference of good and evil. There is tragedy, down to those depths of gloom in which *Troilus and Crēssida* was written; but in the darkness Shakespeare never forgot the existence of light, and by the side of characters like Pandarus and Helen and Ajax, whose worthlessness is more depressing than villainy, created the generous simplicity of Troilus and the wisdom of Ulysses. It is not a question of preaching morals about Shakespearian texts but of simply reading the plays in the spirit in which they were written. To see Lear and Gloucester, Edmund and Regan, Cordelia and Kent as their creator saw them is to share his vision of human good and evil, and to know what he thought first-rate; that in itself is a great education of character. Anyone steeped so deeply in Shakespeare as to absorb him can safely read Wycherley or *Don Juan*, if he wishes to read them. He will have a standard by which to choose and to reject.*

The first-rate in human nature and conduct is present abundantly in history and literature, and we have only to look to see it there. But a further problem arises. Good and bad, corn and tares, grow indiscriminately in these fields. Attila, Caesar Borgia, Richelieu, Frederick the Great, Hitler are in a sense great men: Villon, Boccaccio, the Restoration dramatists are in their way first-rate: yet it is not this kind of excellence that we are seeking, nor should we exhibit as ideals of character and conduct Richelieu and Wolsey, or Heine, Stendhal and Byron, great though they are. Literature and history, like life itself, are a chaos of good and evil, and the evil is mixed with the good. Anyone plunged into this chaos runs great risks. At worst, he may be attracted, infected and corrupted by wrong or false ideals; at least he will be confused and drawn insensibly different ways, growing up with a dissociated personality which lacks unity of spiritual standards and values. The more sensitive and imaginative the character, the greater the danger. That is why Augustine, master of thought and passionate lover of poetry as he was, breaks out into a denunciation of education: 'Woe to thee, stream of human tradition! Who can resist thee? How long wilt thou sweep away the sons of Eve into that vast and stormy sea, which scarcely those who have embarked on the Cross can sail safely?' And again: 'Who can unravel this twisted and tangled skein? It is ugly: let me not look at it.'*

Our aim is to mould character on the principles of what we have come to call Christian civilisation, achieving at lowest the 'natural end of man—virtue and well-being in community'. We must see that we do it, and allow nothing to hamper or defeat our purpose. That raises the difficulty felt by Augustine and the question asked by Plato, which puts the problem clearly and demands a frank answer. 'Youth is the time when the character is being moulded and easily takes any impress one may wish to stamp on it. Then shall we simply allow our children to listen to any stories that anyone happens to make up and so receive into their minds ideas often the very opposite of those we shall think they ought to have when they are grown up?' The problem lies there. It is the biggest problem anyone concerned with education has to answer, for it deals with the greatest task of education. One must not run away from it or let it slip out of mind.†

Shall we expurgate? Expurgation, in any but a limited degree, is impossible. How can history be expurgated? How can brilliant villainy and successful crime be ignored? The difficulty is illustrated by the Bible, where cruelty and love, truth and treachery, high religion and narrow nationalism elbow each other; where the tricks of Jacob, and the extermination of cities are bound in one volume with the Sermon on the Mount; where the word 'blessed' is applied to the merciful, to those who dash their enemies' children against the stones and to Jael who treacherously murdered a fugitive foe. How can such a book be expurgated? Anyone who tries to cut unchristian elements out of the Old Testament will soon despair of his task. And yet what dangers the Bible presents! How often during the ages the devil has cited scripture for his purpose and 'evil souls produced holy witness'! There is point in Oscar Wilde's remark: 'When I think of all the harm that book has done, I despair of ever writing anything to equal it.' The history of religion shows the disastrous effects of reading the Bible without discrimination, and treating the Beatitudes and Samuel's order to kill the Amalekites as if they were equally inspired. But history and literature are sometimes taught much as the Covenanters read the Bible, and as little distinction drawn between the good and evil in them. We must distinguish, though we cannot expurgate.*

History (for our present purpose) is a picture gallery, where we pause longest before the portraits of greatness, learning to distinguish the permanent stars of the human firmament from the meteors, no less brilliant for the moment, which flash across the sky and vanish, and not so dazzled as to confuse greatness with goodness. Between 1770 and 1870 three men changed the face of Europe and altered the course of history—Frederick the Great, Napoleon, and Bismarck. Most readers are dazzled by their genius and achievements and ignore the perhaps more permanent result of their lives—that they impressed on the plastic mind of man a false ideal. Who can measure its corrupting and destructive power? Greatness does not excuse vice or crime, but it enlarges their influence; 'If the light that is in thee be darkness, how great is that darkness.' If there is any truth in the Christian conception of life, if civilisation consists in the advance of justice, mercy and truth, in substituting co-operation for struggle, and a growing sense of the meaning of man's duty to his neighbour, it would have been better for the world if these three great men had never been born; Europe has paid and is paying for their lives in rivers of blood. Their political achievements are well described in Augustine's words: *Remota iustitia quid sunt regna nisi magna latrocinia?* 'Banish justice and what are empires but large-scale brigandage?' We can hold this view without becoming quietists, pacifists or anarchists. Political power, empires, statemen and statesmanship, are not incompatible with justice, as the career of another great man shows, whose life falls within the same period, Abraham Lincoln; or that of President Masaryk, who worked in a smaller field but deserves to be ranked with Lincoln as the ideal democratic statesman. Both are associated with political struggle, and with four years of war. We can measure the gulf separating Lincoln from Frederick the Great and Bismarck—a gulf as wide as that between heaven and hell—by the famous words of the Second Inaugural:

> The Almighty has His own purposes. 'Woe unto the world because of offenses! for it must needs be that offenses come; but woe to that man by whom the offense cometh.' If we shall suppose that American slavery is one of those offenses, which, in the providence of God, must needs come, but which, having continued through His appointed time, He now wills to remove, and that He gives to both North and South this terrible war, as the woe due to those by whom the offense came, shall we discern therein any departure from those divine attributes which the believers in a living God always ascribe to Him? Fondly do we hope—fervently do we pray—that this mighty scourge of war may speedily pass away. Yet, if God wills that it continue until all the wealth piled by the bondman's two hundred and fifty years of unrequited toil shall be sunk, and until every drop of blood drawn with the lash shall be paid with another drawn with the sword, as was said three thousand years ago, so still it must be said, 'The judgments of the Lord are true and righteous altogether.'
>
> With malice toward none; with charity for all; with firmness in the right, as God gives us to see the right, let us strive on to finish the work we are in; to bind up the nation's wounds, to care for him who shall have borne the battle, and for his widow, and his orphan—to do all which may achieve and cherish a just and lasting peace among ourselves, and with all nations.*

Let us then study Frederick, Napoleon and Bismarck, recognise their greatness to the full, and appreciate whatever is good in them and their work, but let us place by their side men like Lincoln and Masaryk, and mark the contrast. If we are told that moral judgments are out of place in the study of history, we can shelter ourselves behind the authority of the greatest of recent English historians, who, well aware of another view, wrote:

> The weight of opinion is against me when I exhort you never to debase the moral currency or to lower the standard of rectitude, but to try others by the final maxim that governs your own lives, and to suffer no man and no cause to escape the undying penalty which history has the power to inflict on wrong. The plea in extenuation of guilt and mitigation of punishment is perpetual. At every step we are met by arguments which go to excuse, to palliate, to confound right and wrong, and reduce the just man to the level of the reprobate....So that we have no common code; our moral notions are always fluid; and you must consider the times, the class from which men sprang, the surrounding influences, the masters in their schools, the preachers in their pulpits, the movement they obscurely obeyed, and so on, until responsibility is merged in numbers, and not a culprit is left for execution. A murderer was no criminal if he followed local custom, if neighbours approved, if he was encouraged by official advisers or prompted by just authority, if he acted for the reason of state or the pure love of religion, or if he sheltered himself behind the complicity of the law. The depression of morality was flagrant; but the motives were those which have enabled us to contemplate with distressing complacency the secret of unhallowed lives.

Unless we follow Acton's maxim, unless we judge, unless we clearly distinguish greatness from goodness, history has as much power to corrupt as to instruct; it ceases to be an instrument of moral education.*

That is true of literature also. There, too, flowers and weeds grow together and some of the flowers are bright but poisonous. It is easier to expurgate literature than history, and almost everyone would agree to some amount of expurgation. Nobody puts into a child's hands books condemned by the law as obscene, nor even every page of the great writers of the world. But there are obvious dangers in expurgation, and they have been put clearly by Cardinal Newman in a lecture to a Catholic University which is one of the best discussions on the subject. He is talking of university education; but *mutatis mutandis* his words apply to schools:

If Literature is to be made a study of human nature, you cannot have a Christian Literature. It is a contradiction in terms to attempt a sinless Literature of sinful men. You may gather together something very great and high, something higher than any Literature ever was; and when you have done so, you will find that it is not Literature at all. You will have simply left the delineation of man, as such, and have substituted for it, as far as you have had anything to substitute, that of man, as he is or might be, under certain special advantages. Give up the study of man, as such, if so it must be; but say you do so. Do not say you are studying him, his history, his mind and his heart, when you are studying something else. Man is a being of genius, passion, intellect, conscience, power. He exercises these various gifts in various ways, in great deeds, in great thoughts, in heroic acts, in hateful crimes....Such is man: put him aside, keep him before you; but, whatever you do, do not take him for what he is not, for something more divine and sacred.*

Literature, then, ceases to be a portrait of man, if everything that falls below Christian standards is eliminated from it; and further, so treated, its study ceases to be a preparation for the life into which its pupils go.

We cannot possibly keep them from plunging into the world, with all its ways and principles and maxims, when their time comes; but we can prepare them against what is inevitable; and it is not the way to learn to swim in troubled waters, never to have gone into them. Proscribe (I do not merely say particular authors, particular works, particular passages) but Secular Literature as such; cut out from your class books all broad manifestations of the natural man; and those manifestations are waiting for your pupil's benefit at the very doors of your lecture room in living and breathing substance. They will meet him there in all the charm of novelty, and all the fascination of genius or of amiableness. To-day a pupil, to-morrow a member of the great world: to-day confined to the Lives of the Saints, to-morrow thrown upon Babel;—thrown on Babel, without the honest indulgence of wit and humour and imagination ever permitted to him, without any fastidiousness of taste wrought into him, without any rule given him for discriminating 'the precious from the vile', beauty from sin, the truth from the sophistry of nature, what is innocent from what is poison. You have refused him the masters of human thought, who would in some sense have educated him because of their incidental corruption. You have shut up from him those whose thoughts strike home to our hearts, whose words are proverbs, whose names are indigenous to all the world, the standard of their mother tongue, and the pride and boast of their countrymen, Homer, Ariosto, Cervantes, Shakespeare, because the old Adam smelt rank in them; and for what have you reserved him? You have given him 'a liberty unto' the multitudinous blasphemy of his day; you have made him free of its newspapers, its reviews, its magazines, its novels, its controversial pamphlets, of its Parliamentary debates, its law proceedings, its platform speeches, its songs, its drama, its theatre, of its enveloping, stifling atmosphere of death.

Ruthless expurgation is a moral danger.*

To expurgate literature is as impossible as to exterminate microbes, but we can take the same measures against its corruptions as we take against microbes. Some of the worst can be destroyed or avoided; we can make people aware of the existence and character of others; and we can immunise human beings from their attack by building up the general health, till it is strong enough to resist infection. 'The mischief', as Newman says, 'is to be met not with argument, not by protests and warnings, but by means of the great counterfascination of purity and truth'. Bring people up in the company of the first-rate, whether in art, thought, morals, or anything else and they will instinctively detect what is inferior. Anyone used to good pictures, good wine, good literature or good men, is not likely to care for bad pictures, bad wine, bad literature or bad men, and needs no further protection than the standard insensibly implanted by living with the first-rate. Reading the poetry of Aeschylus, says a character in Browning, has somehow spoilt my taste for twitterings; and provided that it does not make them conceited or inhuman, men need to have their taste spoilt for twitterings, and most of all in the things that are most important.*

Naturally we read contemporary literature, which mirrors the interests, movements and problems of the day, is easily intelligible, and may include writers destined for immortality. But to read nothing else is to have no standards of comparison, to be narrow and provincial, to risk confusing the ephemeral with the eternal, the cry of the day with the music of the spheres. I saw recently a course of lectures on Housman, Galsworthy, Shaw, Somerset Maugham, James Joyce and others, advertised under the title 'Some authors worth reading'. In one sense the description was justified; all these writers are able craftsmen and in different ways documents on their time. But an equally descriptive title would have been 'Some authors not worth reading'; no one would learn from any of them what, in the full sense of the words, goodness and greatness are. That is one use of reading 'the classics', Greek, Latin or more recent. They give perspective and proportion to our view of our own times; they have a quality of which 'the world is impatient; it chafes against it, rails at it, insults it, hates it; it ends by receiving its influence and undergoing its law. This quality at last inexorably corrects the world's blunders, and procures that the popular poet shall not finally pass for a Pindar, nor the popular historian for a Tacitus, nor the popular preacher for a Bossuet' (Matthew Arnold). These are delusions from which it is better to be free.†

If then we are needing literature to give the vision of what is spiritually first-rate, to form character, and moral standards, we must select what is first-rate in these fields and reject what is not. Some writers are good for our purpose and others are bad, others neutral. If we are looking for the first-rate in ideals and conduct, we shall choose Isaiah, not the Book of Judges; Virgil, not Ovid; Shakespeare, not Marlowe; Milton, not Congreve; Johnson, not Sterne; Shelley, not Byron; George Meredith, not George Moore; Robert Bridges, not A. E. Housman. Even among those writers whom we admit, we shall make a further selection, preferring those—such as Aeschylus and Plato, Shakespeare and Dante—who, of all Europeans, have seen farthest and reached highest and best reveal the greatness of human nature. Then our pupils will see the first-rate and learn the difference between *quod semper, quod ubique, quod ab omnibus,* and *quod aliquando, quod alicubi, quod a nonnullis.* *

'What!' you may say, 'Are we not to read Congreve or *Don Juan* or A. E. Housman, or any other writers whom you put on an arbitrary *Index expurgatorius?* Plato, Shakespeare and Dante, by all means, but why not the others too? They have, in their different degrees, literary power, beauty, genius; and some of them are already ranked among the immortals by the secure verdict of time'.†

Yes, certainly let us read them, but let us realise what we are reading and why. Poetry may be great, yet barren of the highest things in human nature and life. Literary and spiritual excellence are separate things and the one may exist without the other. But, as in history we are dazzled by greatness, so in literature we are dazzled by genius. Greatness in a statesman, genius in a poet are realities with a value of their own and it is perverse to deny their reality and value, but it is equally perverse to let them blind us to the presence of spiritual and moral littleness. Unless either moral goodness, nobility of mind, spiritual greatness are mere words, or literature has no concern with life, writers, like statesmen, should be judged separately, on both counts.

This may sound a platitude, yet in fact we often fail to make the distinction and read unaware of what we are reading. Take, for instance, two popular authors of the last fifty years, Edward Fitzgerald and A. E. Housman. Fitzgerald's *Omar Khayyam* was a favourite with the last generation and read with whole-hearted admiration by many persons who would have been horrified by his view of life, had not their minds been lulled by the sonorous words into unconsciousness of the meaning:

We are no other than a moving row
Of magic Shadow-shapes that come and go
  Round with the Sun-illuminated Lantern held
In Midnight by the Master of the Show;

But helpless Pieces of the Game he plays
Upon this Chequer-board of Nights and Days....

O Thou, who Man of baser Earth didst make,
And even with Paradise devise the Snake:
  For all the Sin wherewith the face of Man
Is blackened—Man's forgiveness give—and take.

How many orthodox Christians have read those lines, fascinated by their stately movement and music and quite unaware of their gloomy determinism, their indictment of theism!*

In this generation the place of Fitzgerald has been taken by A. E. Housman, who has in a higher degree the same qualities of music of words and mastery of form, and a pessimism more self-centred, more self-pitying, with a touch of abjectness which is remote from the dignity and self-restraint of the Victorian writer. Some readers of Housman are probably unaware of his meaning—otherwise his Collected Poems would not be among the books at a School Prize-Day—and more have not fully realised the implications of his view of life. They are too fascinated by his poetry, as poetry, to attend to what he is saying. But that is not true of all his readers, as the experience of an English lecturer in Japan shows:

I thought A. E. Housman would be a good English poet to read. The English is very clear, and it is all a bit gloomy, so I thought they would like it all right. And I like it very much myself, so I thought I'd be able to put it over....I think Housman would have been a good deal shocked by what they made of him. In fact, I am not sure that Housman might not have felt ashamed of himself if he had read those little essays. Because he does literally say what they thought he did, when you come to look at it.... This is what one of them wrote down, almost literally, and most of them took the same line: 'I think Housman is quite right. We will do no good to anyone by dying for our country, but we will be admired and we all want to be admired, and anyway we are better dead.'

The naïve Japanese were no doubt far more ignorant of Housman than their teacher, but they understood him better; and we should imitate them.*

The story may also serve to remind us that we can be poisoned by other things than an overdose of sex. Actually our literature has been less sex-ridden than that of some other countries; the puritanism of the English tradition and perhaps a natural sanity and balance in the English mind have saved us till recently from losing a sense of proportion and allowing a fraction of life to seem its greater part; still more from confusing lust with love. But 'sexual respectability, however important, is not the whole and final concern of life', and literature can be pernicious without being immoral or obscene. The cynicism of *Don Juan* is as ignoble and injurious as any immorality in the poem; the morals of Burns were not much better than Byron's, but his generosity of spirit and sense of goodness are liberal education; while many writers, who would pass the most censorious censor, can corrupt the mind by their attitude to life.†

The same problem—that of choosing one's company—must be faced in literature as in life; it has similar implications and should lead to similar results. 'Will you gossip with your chambermaid or your stable-boy, when you may talk with kings and queens?' There are attractions in the company of stable-boys; they have their own special range of experience and knowledge, and may even be more entertaining and less embarrassing associates than royalty. So, too, with literature. A poet may be a genius, an artist, a master of music and language, and at the same time he may be worthless as a man, or the atmosphere in which he lives may be unhealthy or poisonous. We may read him for his other qualities; though a stable-boy as a man, he may be a king as a writer; but we should realise when he is a stable-boy, and when he is a king. I do not suggest that we should refuse to read writers of modern or ancient times, in whom genius or talent is united with a view of life which we reject; still less that we should read bad poets or writers, because their morals are sound—spiritual excellence does not turn bad poetry into good. I only urge that we should distinguish art and morals, greatness as a poet and greatness as a man; that in reading literature we should be quite clear why we are reading it. Is it for the language or the music, or for the thought? Is it the technique, or the revelation of life that attracts us: beauty, desired because it is beauty and no more, or a beauty in which the highest ranges of human thought and action are revealed? In literature, as in other things, it is possible both to admire and to condemn: and, if we are to have standards in life as well as in art, both are necessary.

Let me sum up. I began by saying that if we are to have a new world, we need human beings to make and live in it, and that we must not leave their education to chance. In the past, men accepted the Christian ideal even if they did not live the Christian life; a child born in the nineteenth century had its mind formed unconsciously by the atmosphere and beliefs around it. There is no such definite formative influence to-day and we must find one. I suggested that education could help to do this, if it showed its pupils the first-rate in life and character as they are revealed in history and literature. All Englishmen should have what Plato wished for his ruling class:

> We would not have our Guardians grow up among representations of moral deformity, as in some foul pasture where, day after day, feeding on every poisonous weed they would, little by little, gather insensibly a mass of corruption in their very souls. Rather we must seek out those craftsmen whose instinct guides them to whatsoever is lovely and gracious; so that our young men, dwelling in a wholesome

climate, may drink in good from every quarter, whence, like a breeze bearing health from happy regions, some influence from noble works constantly falls upon eye and ear from childhood upward, and imperceptibly draws them into sympathy and harmony with the beauty of reason, whose impress they take.*

CHAPTER IV

FROM ATMOSPHERE TO REASON

OUR fundamental need and a chief task of education to-day is to form the right attitude to life and to give what our age lacks, clear values and definite standards. In childhood this must be in the form of an instinctive attitude to life, but not a philosophy of it; an attitude that comes from living with what is first-rate, and so acquiring a sense of it, a love for it, an instinctive repugnance to its opposite. That is as much as can be done in earlier years, as, long ago, Plato saw: 'As for wisdom and firm, true belief, a man is fortunate if he acquires them in advancing years; to possess them with all their attendant blessings is to have reached the full stature of man. But by education I mean goodness in the form in which it is first acquired by a child. If pleasure and pain, liking and dislike, are formed in the soul on right lines before the age of understanding is reached, and if, when that age is attained, these feelings are in concord with reason, thanks to early discipline in the right habits—then this concord, regarded as a whole, is virtue. But if you consider one factor in it, the rightly disciplined attitude to pleasures and pains, by which a man from first to last hates what he should hate and loves what he should love—if you isolate this factor and call it education, you will be giving it its true name.'*

A definite philosophy comes late (Plato thinks 'in advancing years'). Goodness indeed must be acquired by children but acquired in non-rational form, as a habit of feeling pleasure and pain at the right things, hating what should be hated and loving what should be loved. This right feeling comes from early training in the right habits; and this training is the essence of early education—Plato reserves the word education for it; but as people grow up and learn to use their reason, the grounds for these habits are seen and a rational philosophy develops which justifies, explains and fortifies them. It is important that it should develop, for though without the right habits there will be no philosophy or the wrong one, without the philosophy even the best habits are insecure. Atmosphere is transitory, attitudes can change, habits may lose their hold, and none of them have the strength of a rational conviction about life. 'True opinions', as Plato said, 'are a fine thing and their results altogether good, so long as they stay with us; only they will not stay long, but run away out of the human soul, and so they are of little value, unless one fastens them by the tie of cause.' Or, as one might say, an opinion based merely on habit has a shallow foundation which needs to be driven deeper into the firm rock of reason. The vision of goodness in history and literature nourishes goodness in the soul; but the ideals which these subjects contain are at best unsystematic and though they imply a view of life, they do not define or state it, and an education confined to them 'sets up culture in the place of Religion and leaves Religion to be laid waste by the anarchy of feeling'. So in the later years at school the pupil should be at least introduced to a rational philosophy of life. But what philosophy?*

A critic may have already asked on what principle certain men and authors were selected in the last chapter as patterns of the first-rate in human ideals and conduct. Why Socrates, St Bernard, Sir Thomas More, Shaftesbury, Lincoln, Masaryk, rather than Frederick the Great, Napoleon and Bismarck? Why Aeschylus, Plato, Dante, Shakespeare, Shelley, Wordsworth, Robert Bridges, rather than Villon, Marlowe, Congreve, Sterne, Byron, Heine, Stendhal, Housman? It is not a question of mere greatness—if so, the choice, at least in some cases, might have been different—but of what is first-rate in ideals and conduct. And on this latter score, why this selection? On what general principle is it based?

I might reply that it is based on the principle of *quod semper, quod ubique, quod ab omnibus*, that all ages and universal assent would regard most of these men as masters in the art of living. They have outsoared the shadow of our night, and shine beyond question permanent stars of the human firmament. The science, the politics, the commercial and industrial systems, the social life of the age of Aeschylus or Plato or Dante or Shakespeare have passed away and become matters of antiquarian interest, but the writings of these men, mere words, preserved on the most fragile of materials, have survived, as fresh and living as on the day when they were written down. They meet some permanent need not only of their own epoch but of all time, and in a world of change and death possess the secret of immortality. *Securus judicat orbis*; the judgment of the world is hard to challenge, and its judgment on Plato, Dante, Shakespeare and even on Shelley and Wordsworth, is not likely to change.

Is there any common element in these writers, any philosophy discernible in their writings? One's first instinct would be to say 'no'; they are so different, they come from such different peoples, times and civilisations; and most of them are not systematic thinkers or philosophers in the current sense of the word. Yet, whatever their differences, they belong to one family, a strain with strongly stamped characters, which no one could confuse with the other great civilisations of the world, Indian or Chinese: and if we ask what stamped these characters on them, there is only one reply—Greece, Rome, Palestine. Our civilisation, spiritual and intellectual, was born in Greece; Rome applied Greek thought to the life and institutions of a great empire; Christianity added new forces which modified and developed its Graeco-Roman inheritance. We are not Greeks, Romans or Jews, but our air is charged with influences from Greece, Rome and Palestine. However ignorant we may be of them, they will mould us. However we may react from them, we bear their marks. A man may know nothing of Greek thought and literature; he may be an agnostic or an atheist; but Greece, Rome and Christianity have made Western Civilisation, permeate its thought, morals, literature and institutions, and touch its members at every moment of their lives. It is as well, for they are the oxygen in its atmosphere and if they disappeared from it, its life would cease. It is characteristic of the weakness of our education, that most people know nothing of Greece and an increasing number know little of Judaism or Christianity.

The genius of Western civilisation is summed up completely and briefly in the lines:

> Think on the seed ye spring from! Ye were made
> Not to live life of brute beasts of the field,
> But follow virtue and knowledge unafraid.

In the name of this double ideal the Ulysses of Dante calls on his men to venture on the unknown Atlantic; it inspired Bishop Foxe in founding Corpus Christi College, Oxford, in 1516, and appears in the preamble to his Statutes as the aim of higher education:

> We have no abiding city here, but we seek one to come in heaven, at which we hope to arrive with the greater ease and despatch, if while we travel in this life, we rear a ladder whereby we may gain a readier ascent. We give the name of virtue to the right side of the ladder, and that of knowledge to the left...

The words reveal their origin; ἀρετή and ἐπιστήμη inspired the life and thought of Ancient Greece, passed thence into the vocabulary of Europe, and gave our civilisation the double but indivisible ideal of virtue and knowledge. The word virtue was continually reinterpreted: but we recognise *idées mères* of our own civilisation in the cardinal virtues of Plato—Wisdom, Courage, Temperance and Justice, and in the longer list of Aristotle which adds to these Intelligence, Moral Insight, Liberality, Munificence, High-Mindedness, Right Ambition, Good Temper, Friendliness, Truth, Just Resentment, Modesty. Christianity, in the Beatitudes and elsewhere in the New Testament, but most of all in the life of its Founder, modified and added to, but did not supersede this vision of human goodness, a composite yet harmonious ideal which inspires and pervades Western civilisation and gives it amid all its differences a certain unity of direction. Therefore, in education, to form the growing mind and character, we shall choose writers and men who are most permeated by this ideal and in whom it appears at its purest and greatest, not those in whom it is diluted or distorted or who are in rebellion or reaction against it; Lincoln and Masaryk, not Napoleon or Bismarck or Hitler; Plato, Dante, Shakespeare, Shelley, Wordsworth, not Marlowe, Stern, Byron, Heine. Here is the main stream of the river, here is the current which leads to the sea, and here the boats of youth must be launched, not in back-eddies and side-streams.*

I have now implicitly answered the question asked above—to what philosophy our education should lead, when we pass from atmosphere to a reasoned view of life, and floating influences and impressions crystallise into a rational conviction. It will be the philosophy which lies behind that atmosphere and those influences. If Greek thought and Christianity created the soul of Western civilisation, formed its mind and are the vitamins in its life-blood, then these are the philosophies for which we are looking, and before his education is completed everyone should have an idea what they are. Many people never realise the connection between them; some even oppose them to each other. But in history and in Christian thought the two are linked indissolubly. Christianity surviving from the downfall of the ancient world salved and adapted Roman organisation and Greek thought, and incorporated both in the new house that it built for Western civilisation. The West owes to Greece the conclusions about God and conduct which the human mind reached without revelation and which we call natural religion and natural morals (is there any nobler or more concise expression of the latter than Plato's words 'Goodness is the health, beauty and well-being of the soul; evil is its disease, deformity and weakness'). A knowledge of these should enter into any scheme of higher education, so that people can enter life with a reasoned philosophy of it and not merely with good habits.*

Some people may wonder why I suggest that the best introduction to natural religion and morals is through Greek thought, and that every educated person should have an acquaintance with it. The answer is partly given in some words of T. H. Green. From Socrates and his followers

> comes the connected scheme of virtues and duties within which the educated conscience of Christendom still moves, when it is impartially reflecting on what ought to be done.... The articulated scheme of what the virtues and duties are, in their difference and in their unity, remains for us now in its main outlines what the Greek philosophers left it....Once for all they conceived and expressed the conception of a free or pure morality, as resting on what we may venture to call a disinterested interest in the good; of the several virtues as so many applications of that interest to the main relations of social life; of the good itself not as anything external to the capacities virtuously exercised in its pursuit, but as their full realisation....When we come to ask ourselves what are the essential forms in which, however otherwise modified, the will for true good (which is the will to be good) must appear, our answer follows the outlines of the Greek classification of the virtues. It is the will to know what is true, to make what is beautiful; to endure pain and fear, to resist the allurements of pleasure (i.e. to be brave and temperate), if not, as the Greek would have said, in the service of the state, yet in the interest of some form of human society; to take for oneself, to give to others, of those things which admit of being given and taken, not what one is inclined to but what is due.†

Not only did the Greeks create the theory of natural morals, but their exposition of it has certain advantages over any other. They produced, in the *Republic* of Plato and the *Ethics* of Aristotle, two text-books on morals, which are unlike other text-books in being writen by men of genius. Further, they have a simplicity and directness which belong to pioneers and are impossible to a later age. 'The Greeks', said Nietzsche, 'are simple, like genius; that is why they are the immortal teachers.'

No one begins to study the geography of a district on a six-inch-to-the-mile map; he starts with one of smaller scale, which shows main features in clear relief and omits confusing detail. It is equally foolish to commence the study of morals or politics either on large maps of them or on inferior small ones. In every subject the most exhaustive book is the worst for the beginner; and if he is sensible, he chooses one which will fix in his mind essential points and main problems, before he proceeds to complications and refinements. Because they are such books, the *Republic*, the *Ethics* and the *Politics* are incomparable introductions to moral and political questions.

If I were asked what knowledge of Greek thought might reasonably be given in the later school years, I would suggest that the pupil should at least be introduced, if possible to Aristotle, and certainly to Socrates, Plato and the Stoics and to the conception of *areté*, which runs like a gold thread through the achievement of Greece. There is no equivalent for the word *areté* in English, though there is plenty of the thing in English life. It is 'virtue' not in the modern but in the old sense of the word; 'excellence' with no moral sense necessarily attaching to it. Everything, the Greeks said, has a use, a function, a virtue of which it is capable. Take things as different as a knife, an eye, a doctor. Each of them has a use and is capable of a virtue. A knife's use is to cut, an eye's to see, a doctor's to keep or make us well; and their virtue is achieved when they fulfil their use and function. If they do this, we call them good, if they fail, they are bad—as knives, eyes, doctors. Hence, the task and problem of each of them is to fulfil its function and so achieve its virtue. It is an argument in which it is difficult to see a flaw.

But what is true of knives and eyes, is true, the Greeks thought, of men also. they too must have a function, a use, a virtue of which they are capable and which it is their business to achieve; and in so far as they achieve it, we shall call them good. It is easier to see the function and virtue of an eye or a knife than of a man: and in fact he has many functions, and therefore many virtues to strive after. A human being is a member of a family—as son or daughter, husband or wife, father or mother; he is a citizen, a member of a state; he has a profession or occupation; in each of these roles he has a different function, and in each function is capable of a virtue, and excellence, which consists in doing the particular job well, in being a good son or daughter, a good citizen, good in his occupation—whether it is that of Prime Minister or of shop assistant. He, no less than the knife or the eye, is judged by the way in which, in each particular capacity, he does the job in question well. But that is not enough. Man is more than a citizen, a parent or child, a person with an occupation; he is also a human being and in that capacity, too, is capable of a virtue. As a human being he has a body, an intellect and a character, and his business is to make the most of each of these, and see that all three are developed to the excellence of which they are capable, used rightly and used to the full. He must aim at *areté*, at virtue, in all.

This was the clue which the Greeks followed through the labyrinth of life. Its business, they thought, is to seek the highest and make the most, of whatever a man is or does. They admired every kind of virtue, of excellence, sought after them and tried to create a society in which they could be achieved: and this ideal, this purpose partly explains why in so many fields of life they achieved an excellence which, long after they have perished, remains a model and an inspiration.

There may be better ends, but this is not a mean one, and it is simple, intelligible, convincing and practical. It leaves money in the right place. It is a perpetual challenge in hours of doubt, weariness, slackness, pessimism. It is a philosophy consistent with Christianity; only, where Plato and Aristotle thought, not unplausibly, that the Reason was the noblest thing in man, and the highest life, therefore, the life of the Reason as lived by poets, artists, philosophers and men of science, St Paul has a different conception of the highest virtue, and has expounded his view of human excellence in the 13th chapter of the first Epistle to the Corinthians. The Greek ideal may seem too impersonal to English minds. Yet among all peoples it is the motive force in the creative artist, who seeks perfection for its own sake through language, or paint, or stone, or sound: and outside the ranks of artists, many people are driven on by it to do in their special field the best work of which they are capable. In it there is something, which lies at the heart of all morals, the passionate desire for good, simply because it is good.*

The ideal of *areté* is a moral philosophy in itself, and this conception of excellence as something to be sought in every sphere and activity is a valuable corrective to our narrower idea of virtue. Apart from it, every educated person ought to have some knowledge of certain individual Greek thinkers. Socrates, Plato, Aristotle, and Epictetus and Marcus Aurelius among the Stoics, are the most important for our purpose, in themselves and because of their influence on the world, and every pupil after the age of seventeen, who is capable of receiving it, should be given some idea of them; of Socrates for the example of his life and the stimulus and intellectual discipline of his thought, of Plato, because he is not only one of the great religious thinkers of the world but also in the direct line that leads to Christianity. 'Every problem which Plato discusses is still alive to-day.'†

Aristotle is more difficult. His influence on human thought has been enormous, though different from Plato's. In morals and in politics, as in natural history, his approach to a subject is scientific and inductive. But his gritty style and prosy manner are not attractive, and though there are many translations of his *Ethics* (some extremely bad), there is as yet none with notes for English readers. Still the *Ethics* is one of the great books of the world: it propounds a clear, rational, noble view of the art of living; and it is fascinating and stimulating to take his list of the separate virtues, and his detailed account of each, and compare these with our own views on the subject, seeing where we should agree or differ, where we have gone beyond Aristotle, and where we can learn from him.††

But, it will be said, do you expect everyone to learn Greek, and are you not adding an enormous subject to an overcrowded curriculum? The answer to both these questions is 'No'. For anyone interested in literature and language to be ignorant of Greek is a great loss, but obviously only a small number of persons will learn it. But the others can easily make the acquaintence of Greek thought in the translations. Nor does the programme suggested here demand much time; though it contains nourishment for a life-time, its bulk is small. There is no question of an elaborate study of Plato, still less of the Stoics, whose moral thought alone concerns us. Half-a-dozen books on the shelves of the school library and effective encouragement to read them, in or out of school hours, open the door to a great world.*

In history and in thought Greece leads on to Christianity, and the teaching of this in schools raises the so-called problem of religious teaching. It is not too much to say that the spiritual future of this country depends on its right solution and on the solution being carried rightly into practice. In the last nineteen centuries Christianity has been the greatest new fact in the history of Europe, which is unintelligible without some knowledge of it. It meets us in every stage and phase of our civilisation since the first century A.D., in politics and social life, in thought, literature, art, music, architecture. You may think it a deplorable incident in the development of man, but to anyone ignorant of it Western civilisation is a tapestry from which half the pattern has been cut out. Incidentally, its 'book' is both the finest monument of the English language and the greatest book in the world. Thus, quite apart from any religious reasons, some knowlege of Christianity must be given in education.

That raises the question what should be taught. Religious education is not a question of knowing the dates and authorship of the books of the Bible, or the meaning of phrases like 'the abomination of desolation', but of seeing Christianity as a way of living, as a life that was actually lived. The first and most important thing in it is the 'actual portrait, preserved in the Synoptic Gospels, of a carpenter's son who, gathering some followers round him, taught, healed, and lived his life in Palestine, and was crucified by the Roman authorities. To see Christ so is to see Him as His contemporaries saw Him in Galilee and in Judaea during His earthly life; to see what convinced the men closest to Him and who knew Him best, that he was not an ordinary man but the Son of God, convincing them not as

> Light half-believers of a casual creed,

but so that they never hesitated for a moment to change their lives and to die for their conviction. That conviction of a few Jewish peasants in a minor dependency of the great and highly civilised Roman Empire seemed to most of its citizens an extravagant folly, but persisted as the Empire, apparently so stable and permanent, fell into collapse, and outlived every other creed and philosophy of the Graeco-Roman world. Thus much everyone must admit. It is a mere matter of fact. The facts recorded in the Gospels do not exhaust Christianity, but they are, in the witness of St John's Gospel, the most important part of it. 'These things are written that ye might believe that Jesus is the Christ, the Son of God; and that believing ye may have life through His name.' To expound these facts, though it is not to teach Christianity, is to give the premises for it. It is to give more of it than was ever given to some of us in what were regarded as Christian schools. And anyone given so much has seen the Christian life, and the grounds of the Christian faith.'*

This should lead to a knowledge of the Christian theory of life. The Life leads to the Creed. So it was in the history of Christianity, where the Creed was a late growth, a belief to which the actual experience of Christians led, and which embodied that experience but did not precede it: the Nicene Creed was formulated 300 years after Christ's death; the

Apostles' Creed is not earlier than the middle of the second century and received its final formulation much later. The individual should travel by the same road as the early Christian community: he should arrive at the Creed, not start from it; and it will mean infinitely more to him, if he comes to it, as the early Christians did, as a rational account of facts which he knows and of an experience which he has had. That indeed is the road by which most, if not all, people do travel: they come to accept the Creed because after living and thinking it seems to them the most rational account of the facts of history and of their own experience; they may, of course, learn it at any age or stage but so learnt it is inert knowledge; only personal experience will bring it to life. That is the regular process and right method in all education—first practice, then theory; first the facts, then the formulation of a principle to explain them: 'education is the drawing and directing of youth towards that right reason which the law affirms and the experience of the eldest and best has affirmed to be right.'*

This is not to say that we can at any stage dispense with dogma. Some dogma is inevitable. To say that the teaching of Jesus, or any of it, conveys the truth about life, is a highly dogmatic statement, implying a very definite view about the universe and human nature; to say that the teaching is false or valueless is equally dogmatic; and it is also dogmatic to say that we cannot form an opinion on the matter but must suspend our judgment. Agnosticism, like theism or atheism, is dogmatic and there is no credit, least of all any intellectual credit, in halting between two opinions, when in fact you must *act* as if one or the other was true. Only a people with the English indifference to logic could have orginated and approved an attempt to find an intellectual excuse for not making up the mind in matters where action is inevitable, and where any action implies a theory of conduct. Agnosticism enables English intellectuals conscientiously to indulge in the national vice of keeping thought and action apart, and concealing from the right hand what the left hand does.

How much dogma should be taught at school? The following suggestion by Professor L. A. Reid of Newcastle is worth our consideration:

There is one (and only one) living God, the Author and Sustainer of the universe, whose nature is wisdom and love. Whilst the existence and nature of God can be apprehended in many ways (e.g. through thought in philosophy and scientific activity, or experience of beauty in nature and in art, through friendship and community of every kind and through suffering and joy), the Christian believes the nature and love of God to have been as completely embodied and revealed as it is possible for it to be revealed in a single human being, in the person, teaching, life and death of Christ. Not through his teaching alone (Christianity can never be reduced to a code of ethics) but through the quality of his life itself and in the manner of his death the Christian believes to be shown the very nature of God, of self-sacrificing love. The true and only true way of man's life he believes to be founded upon humble submission and confession before God. The Christian believes that only through the apprehension of the love of God and in freely given submission to His will can he properly understand the love of brother-man, and the Brotherhood of Man becomes a reflection of the Fatherhood of God. Christianity is humanistic but not merely humanistic. It believes that the sanctity and the equality of human beings are not *ultimately* human attributes but are derived from the purpose of God. And finally, this view of life is one which views ultimate reality not as material, but as spiritual and in some sense eternal.

Such a statement is of course very incomplete, and of course it would not be taught in this abstract form to childern. It is a sort of 'jumping-off ground' for further thought and experience. It is a minimum, and as far as possible it avoids speculations. It asserts, for example, that the nature of God is revealed in Christ, but it does not attempt to formulate *how*.

It may be added that, whereas the Creed is composed of historical and theological affirmations, which do not explicitly demand any particular conduct though no doubt they imply it, this statement stresses Christianity as a gospel of action and points definitely to the kind of action which it requires. That is an advantage; for

Christianity is too often regarded, both by those who profess it and those who reject it, as an intellectual belief and not as a way of life; in teaching it is important to stress the latter aspect.*

On some of these points there may be disagreement, but there can be no doubt that higher education is incomplete without some knowledge of Hellenism and of Christianity (to put these in their chronological order). If we were Indians or Chinese, it might be otherwise; but our origin and traditions are different; we can learn from the East but we belong to the civilisation of the West and shall neither understand nor master it, if we are ignorant of the rock from which we are hewn. Without some knowledge of Hellenism and Christianity men go into the world having, at best, a partial and inadequate view of human greatness and goodness, and lacking a clear idea how life should be lived. With it, we shall have met men at their highest and we shall know the two great European interpretations of the nature and destiny of man. The spirit, design and aim of Western civilisation will become clear, and we can follow it with intelligence, and some hope of success.

I quoted earlier Mr Lippmann's criticism of American education, which describes a condition to which we are tending, if indeed we have not already reached it. The following passage from his lecture is equally worth our consideration:

> It is said that since the invention of the steam engine we live in a new era, an era so radically different from all preceding ages that the cultural tradition is no longer relevant, is in fact misleading. I submit to you that this is a rationalisation, that this is a pretended reason for the education void which we now call education. The real reason, I venture to suggest, is that we reject the religious and classical heritage, first, because to master it requires more effort than we are willing to compel ourselves to make, and, second, because it creates issues that are too deep and too contentious to be faced with equanimity. We have abolished the old curriculum because we are afraid of it, afraid to face any longer in a modern democratic society the severe discipline and the deep, disconcerting issues of the nature of the universe, and of man's place in it and of his destiny....Modern

education has renounced the idea that the pupil must learn to understand himself, his fellow men and the world in which he is to live as bound together in an order which transcends his immediate needs and his present desires. As a result the modern school has become bound to conceive the world as a place where the child, when he grows up, must compete with other individuals in a struggle for existence. And so the education of his reason and of his will must be designed primarily to facilitate his career. By separating education from the classical-religious tradition the school cannot train the pupil to look upon himself as an inviolable person because he is made in the image of God. These very words, though they are the noblest words in our language, now sound archaic. The school cannot look upon society as a brotherhood arising out of a conviction that men are made in a common image. The teacher has no subject matter that even pretends to deal with the elementary and universal issues of human destiny. The graduate of the modern school knows only by accident and by hearsay whatever wisdom mankind has come to in regard to the nature of men and their destiny....The emancipated democracies have renounced the idea that the purpose of education is to transmit Western culture. Thus there is a cultural vacuum, and this cultural vacuum was bound to produce, in fact it has produced, progressive disorder. For the more men have become separated from the spiritual heritage which binds them together, the more has education become egoist, careerist, specialist and asocial.

These words accurately diagnose the disease of Western civilisation and suggest its cure.*

'But', someone may object, 'these are the methods of Hitler. Your ideal may lead in a different direction, but it has the same character. You wish to form the childish mind, when it is powerless to resist, to impose a view of life on it, to ignore its right to freedom. You will destroy the plant, so rare, delicate and precious in the human garden—the desire to see things as they are and to follow the argument where it leads. And in the end your fate will be the nemesis of dictatorship—death of intellectual integrity and of anything that can be called intellectual life.' No doubt there is a danger here but there is sufficient latitude even in the individuals and authors suggested for study in the previous chapter (who are in any case only specimens taken from a much longer available list of suitable models) to avoid any risk of narrow outlook. Aeschylus, Plato, Virgil, Dante, Shakespeare, Milton, Goethe, Shelley, Wordsworth have indeed something common in their fundamental attitude to life, but a mind formed by their study is not likely to be one-sided or blind. There would be more justice in the criticism that a standard derived from them would be a Least Common Multiple so vague that no one would be offended by it but no one helped.

But when a critic speaks of the danger in forming the growing mind, I am inclined to ask him: 'And you, do you not impose a view of life on your child? Do you allow him to grow up dirty in person and habits, greedy, cruel, a liar, an egotist living for himself? Do you say to him: some people think that might is right and that the strong should take what they can and the weak suffer what they must; others think that life is a quest for pleasure and the wise man evades any duty to his state or his neighbour and tries to live tranquil and undisturbed with his friends; make up your mind on these points, I express no opinion about them? Do you bring him up to believe that there is no distinction between right and wrong? But if so, are you not arbitrarily deciding the biggest of all questions? When you come to history, do you leave your child to suppose that Hitler is as good a model as Abraham Lincoln, that burning heretics is a sound method of propagating religion, that in the Industrial Revolution the champions of laissez-faire may have been right and their opponents wrong? Judgments on these points are more than a condemnation of persons and facts; they imply and rest on a definite view of life.' The fact is that the firmest believer in freedom moulds, or, if we prefer the phrase, tyrannises over, the mind of his child and takes liberty from it in the cradle.

It is fortunate that most people do try to implant a view of life in their children, for if they do not teach, the world does. Every film and newspaper and novel teaches. Every advertisement page, every platform on the Underground Railway preaches a sermon on the Virtue of Acquisitiveness. 'Here', they say, 'are goods necessary to your happiness, beer, motor-cars, whisky, cigarettes, permanent waves, 'collars for discerning men'. All can be bought for money; if you have money, they are yours—collars, whiskies, motor-cars, permanent waves.' The advertisers have no qualms in enforcing their doctrine, no objectivity, no respect for delicate consciences, no interest or scruple about effects on character. They have something to sell and mean to sell it, and though they may not believe in Latin, their motto has been written in words of Horace which describe and denounce a Roman weakness:

Rem facias, rem;
Si possis, recte; si non, quocunque modo rem:

'Make money, money; rightly, if you can; if not, by any means, money.'*

This hoarse clamour drowns the low voices of right values, reason, even of commonsense; the more important to make those voices ring in the ears of youth. Even so they may grow faint in later life.

For we exaggerate the power of teaching to fix the human mind unalterably. Jesuits may have claimed to be able to do it in the first seven years of life; yet not all their pupils have died good Catholics. Recent psychology has talked in the same strain, but the latest pronouncement on a subject is not the same thing as the last word on it. Facts point another way. Do children brought up well in good homes always grow into good men; have none of us discarded views in which as children we were carefully indoctrinated? Personally, I was brought up in a conservative atmosphere and regarded Gladstone as an incarnation of evil; to-day, I am a liberal, and should look to the future more happily if I saw a modern Gladstone among our politicans. Most people have similar experiences. Liberty has outlived many tyrannies, and human nature, or rather human reason, has a way of asserting itself; *expellas furca, tamen usque recurret*; and perhaps the most constant law of human conduct is that extremes always produce reaction. The discipline of the Mediaeval Church is followed by the license of the Renaissance, the rule of the Saints by the Restoration Drama, the Classicism of the eighteenth century by the Romantic Revival, the photographic art of the nineteenth century by Surrealism and Cubism. The contemporaries of Tennyson could see no defects in him, their successors no merits. In one age human beings walk on the right side of the road; in the next they will be found in the ditch on the left. The one thing, alas! which they cannot do is to keep in the centre. And the danger, such as it is, of dominating a pupil's mind becomes negligible when the teacher is aware of it, believes in truth and has a respect for human personality; as he must if he has any respect either for Hellenism or for Christianity.*

In the past totalitarianism and tyranny might conceivably have suppressed permanently any views but their own. In fact, they have not done so. The invention of printing, while it has given dictators new weapons of great immediate effect, has enormously reduced their ultimate power. The Emperor Domitian was wise when, having executed the republican leaders, he destroyed their writings. 'His savagery attacked not only the authors but even their books, and the triumvirs were assigned the duty of burning in the Forum these memorials of illustrious talent. Presumably Domitian thought that those flames destroyed the voice of the Roman people, the freedom of the Senate, the moral consciousness of mankind; he went on to expel from Rome the teachers of philosophy and drove into exile all liberal teaching, to prevent any trace of goodness meeting his eyes.' Domitian's attempt to exterminate adverse thought might have succeeded before printing existed. It failed; to-day it would be hopeless. Literature—in the first century A.D. a small river—has grown, partly through the natural additions to it, partly through its dissemination by printing, into a vast ocean where all the thoughts which have crossed the mind of man through three millennia can be found, swimming on the surface or easily dredged up from the depths. Here, in countless forms, are conservatism, liberalism, communism, anarchy; atheism, agnosticism, religion in its many forms; every system of morals, every view of life or of the state. This ocean is round us and no one can hold the human spirit back from sounding in its depths—the human spirit, unquiet and curious, and grown still more so, since the day when Eve made her decision and accepted the serpent's offer; 'your eyes shall be opened, and ye shall be as gods, knowing good and evil'.*

But it is as important to distinguish good and evil as to know them: and, at least for educated persons in the democratic countries, this is the real problem. Our danger is not too few but too many opinions; not to be penned in a single belief but to be puzzled by innumerable alternatives; not a closed mind but an irresolute one; to drift unanchored from one station to another, from deeps to shallows, from safe water to the rocks; an incapacity to refuse the evil and choose the good. A major task of education is to help to the right choice.

CHAPTER V

TWO DRAGONS IN THE ROAD

STANDARDS, right values, the science of good and evil—to implant these is an essential part of education. Many forces thwart this work, but two of the most serious hindrances to it are examinations and specialisation.

The examination system is both an opiate and a poison. It is an opiate because it lulls us into believing that all is well when most is ill. 'Look', the public says, 'at this list of scholarships; see how many children have got their School Certificate: something is clearly happening; the school is doing its job'. Something no doubt is happening; but it may not be education: it may be the administration of a poison which paralyses or at least slows down the natural activities of the healthy mind. The healthy human being, finding himself a creature of unknown capacities in an unknown world, wants to learn what the world is like, and what he should be and do in it. To help him in answering these questions is the one and only purpose of education. But that is not the prime aim of the ordinary pupil who is working for a School or Higher Certificate or for a scholarship or a degree, and for whom the examination becomes much more important than seeing 'visions of greatness', and 'getting through' excuses all shortcomings and disguises all omissions. I am speaking here throughout of external examinations, not of those set by the school, as tests of progress, which are useful and necessary. Examinations are harmless when the examinee is indifferent to their result, but as soon as they matter, they begin to distort his attitude to education and to conceal its purpose. The more depends on them, the worse their effect. For disinterestedness is the essence of all good education, and liberal education is impossible without it.

It is not suggested that nothing is learnt and no education received in working for an examination; that would be obviously untrue. But, to recur to my previous metaphor, the examination system is a poison which slows down education in most cases and in some paralyses it, and no one wholly escapes its bad effects. The slow or stupid child suffers most, since preparing for the ordeal occupies more of its time and mind; and for some intelligent but nervous children examinations become an obsession. But the keenest student knows the sense of relief when he finishes his last examination and feels himself free to read and study what interests him simply because it is intersting, without any thought of what he is 'expected to know' or 'what may be set'. The blinkers are gone; he can look round with unrestricted eyes; and he knows how the young Athenian felt who answered Socrates' question whether they should pursue a certain intellectual inquiry: 'Should we, do you say? Are there any pleasures worth living for like these?'*

It is not only the pupil but—and this is far more serious—the teacher, who finds his energies and attention drawn from education to examination needs. No doubt there are schools and teachers which resist the insidious pressure, teach their subject for its interest and for nothing else and burn no incense on the examination altar. But the pressure is hard. Most people judge a school by its examination results. Its reputation, however well-established, is affected by them; and a school with a name to make or competitors to face has an overpowering temptation to commend itself to the world by obtaining as many Scholarships and School and Higher Certificates as possible. Such results are intelligible to Boards of Governors and to the general public, and are generally expected by them. The teacher is tempted to show his competence by securing a big list of awards, the headmaster is tempted to demand them in the interest of the school:

Things done, that took the eye and had the price,
O'er which, from level stand,
The low world laid its hand
Found straightway to its mind, could value in a trice.

And, apart from this, however idealistic headmaster or teacher may be, they must reflect that a pupil's future in life may depend on an examination result and that their duty is to see that he is successful.

Any evils that might follow from the disappearance of examinations are nothing to the harm they do. They are in fact a refined form of the old and now universally condemned system of 'payment by results'; but whereas under it the payment was a money grant to the school, under the examination system it takes the form of prestige to the school and to the pupil, and (in the case of scholarships) a money payment to the latter. The examination system has the same bad effect on education as that produced by 'payment by results'. A historian of English education describes the effect of 'payment by results' as follows: 'The "results" procured were far too frequently mechanical results. It encouraged the neglect of the moral and other spiritual factors which constitute the most valuable parts of all education.' He goes on to point out that the system restricted the field of education by causing schools to concentrate on 'profitable' subjects. Each of these charges can be brought against examinations. They procure 'far too frequently mechanical results'. They encourage 'the neglect of the moral and other spiritual factors which constitute the most valuable parts of education'. 'Subjects can have meaning only as they are treated as aspects of active and living human experience. Whether, if considered from this point of view, they can continue to be examinable in the traditional manner is at least an open question.' It is as impossible to examine in the most vital parts of education as to anatomize life on a dissecting table, and therefore the pressure of examinations continually pushes them into the background or out of sight. Further, it tends to restrict education to the subjects of the examination in question, with disastrous results in the case of examinations for university scholarships. I recently asked two mathematical scholars at Oxford who came from different schools how much time they had given during their last school year to other subjects than science and mathematics. In both cases the answer was 'one hour a week'. What an education: bad for the scholarship winners, but they at least had their reward; worse still for those whose education had been narrowed to win a scholarship and who failed to win one! I asked one of the latter class, who had tried unsuccessfully for a scholarship in science, what proportion of his time had been given to other subjects. The answer was 'six periods out of forty-two in the week'. It transpired that the only English literature read in the small time allotted to other subjects than his specialisation was Ibsen's *Ghosts*, a work presumably selected for its supposed connection with science, and considered to be English literature because it had been translated into English. Contrast with this miserable education the training given before the last war in the *Oberrealschule*, the secondary school in which the future scientists of Germany were educated, and in which less than half the time was allotted to science and mathematics: in the highest class eleven periods out of thirty-one were given to them, and the rest to other subjects.*

Unfortunately there is a risk of the importance of examinations increasing. Already, when a boy's parents cannot afford to send him to a secondary school or a university, his whole life may depend on an examination result, and this is bad for him and for education. However disinterested he or his teacher may be, neither can forget what is at stake. As a boy of twelve I was a candidate for an Eton scholarship (which I failed to get), but my chief memories of the episode are of the roast mutton in College Hall and of eating strawberries in the playing fields. That is the right spirit in which to take an examination. My feelings at the time and my surviving memories would have been very different if my future had depended on getting a scholarship. But the number of people who will be able to take examinations in a light-hearted way seems likely to decrease.

We are moving from a society where men as a whole have been born to a certain condition of life and normally have accepted it, to a society, based as we hope on justice, where everyone will find the place to which his character and abilities entitle him. Well and good. But how easily such a society may become acutely competitve! Everyone must find his right place, everyone will desire to find it, and, unless human nature changes, will wish his place to be as high as possible. What possibilities of intense competition that suggests! And how will he find his place? How but by examination? And if so, education becomes a savage competitive system. It ceases to be education and becomes a road to a career. Shakespeare is read, not because he is Shakespeare, but because he is an examination subject in a syllabus, and the child who reads him sees behind the figures of Cordelia or Juliet or Hamlet or Lear the possibility of an examination question which may admit him to the university and determine the course of his life.

We should therefore adapt the wording of a historic motion in the House of Commons and resolve that the influence of examinations has increased, is increasing, and ought to be diminished, and in pursuance of this principle we should restrict their power and as far as possible use the school record and the interview as a substitute or part-substitute. It is impossible to get rid of them altogether; they are inevitable, I am afraid, for university scholarships and for primary university degrees, and in cases where a small selection has to be made out of a large number of candidates. Here we must endure what we must and minimise what we can. But it is difficult to see any conclusive reason why the most baneful of them, the School Certificate, should exist. It does most damage, because it affects most children and distorts secondary education almost from the first. If we are told that some business men believe that a School Certificate is better evidence of a child's capacities than its school record and its teacher's testimonial we must reply that the education of thousands of children ought not to be spoilt each year for such a superstition. The School Certificate had its uses when it was first instituted. It replaced a multitude of external examinations; the standard of teaching in some schools was low, and an external examination imposed on all schools was the best way of raising its level. To-day its work has been done; standards have been raised and established; and, under adequate inspection and with a prescribed curriculum education may be allowed to replace the examination. To say that without it the teacher cannot teach, and that the pupil will not learn, is to insult both and to ignore facts. Elementary and technical schools can do their work without the spur of an examination. Why should it be indispensable in secondary schools?*

The second dragon in the path of true education is specialisation, which normally begins at sixteen. Life is more specialised than it was and more special knowledge is needed to live it competently. Further, limited specialisation after sixteen is educationally beneficial. But it has dangers, and it becomes disastrous when, in fact if not in theory, it excludes the wider human and spiritual interests, when these are ignored and slowly atrophied, when the pupil becomes a mere scientist or mathematician, a mere historian or modern linguist or classic. Then the adolescent suffers from the disease that so often attacks the man who is absorbed in his special occupation and becomes a mere industrialist, a mere economist, a mere civil servant, a mere grocer or artisan. Though there is plenty of materialism in England, the English are not fundamentally materialists. But the specialist tendency in education leads to materialism in effect, though not in intention. A boy takes to modern languages because they will be 'useful in after life', or to chemistry and physics because he intends to enter industry; or he must read the pre-registration subjects at school, so that he can start his full medical course at the university. Unless care is taken, the whole atmosphere of his education changes; the stress is on vocation, not on education; the liberal, human, spiritual element gives way to practical need and material advantage. The danger of specialisation varies with the subject. Some subjects imply, if they do not impart, a spiritual view of life; some subjects do not—or do so in a limited and inadequate way or to an infinitesimal extent. Over-specialisation in mathematics and science is, from this point of view, the more dangerous. It is indeed deplorable if students in languages, literature and history have no chance of at least keeping in touch with science through their secondary school course. To know nothing of science is to be, so far, intellectually maimed. But the background of their studies is human conduct and human ideals. What else is the subject of literature and history? The subject of science is different; it deals with the material world and material aspects of man; the rest of him—that is nine-tenths of him—is not its business. Over-specialisation in it tends to produce scientists who are admirable technicians but no more, and who therefore lack the influence outside their subject, which its importance and the interest of the community demands.

Specialism is bad at school; it increases at the university. If Professor Whitehead is right in saying that 'moral education is impossible without the habitual vision of greatness', then the moral education of most persons becomes of little importance when they have obtained a School Certificate, and practically ceases when they reach the university, where the student is absorbed in science or economics or some other specialism, and is often unconscious that there is anything else in the world, just as in later life and on a lower level some men are absorbed in making money, equally unaware of other aims or interests. But the quality of a civilisation does not depend only on its science, economics or sociology but even more on its standards, values, ideals, its sense of what is first-rate in life, its religion. We act too often as if these, so far as education is concerned, belong to a period that ends with the school, or at latest the Higher Certificate, and when these have been passed, feel that we have done enough and can safely settle down to the serious business of medicine or science or economics or sociology.*

This disastrous practice has actually been erected into a principle by Professor Dewey, whose influence on American education has been great and in some ways unfortunate, and who urges 'the demarcation of secondary work as the period of general training and culture, thus making it to the period of the knowledge of self in relation to the larger meanings of life; and the reservation of the higher institution for specific training, for gaining control of the particular body of knowledge and methods of research which fit the individual to apply truth to the guidance of his own special calling in life'. There speaks the voice of an age concentrated on means and indifferent to ends. Shrouded in the decent obscurity of Professor Dewey's English, his theory may shock us less than if it was exposed naked in plan language, but in effect it says: 'when your secondary education ends, you can drop culture and the "larger meanings of life": philosophy, history, literature are done with (unless of course you are specialising in them, when you will approach them as a "body of knowledge" for which special methods of research are required); you will have solved their problems and penetrated their mysteries; dismiss them and absorb yourself in your profession.'†

An admirable description of our practice, but how disastrous an ideal! As if there was any 'period' for 'the knowledge of self in relation to the larger meanings of life'; as if this knowledge could be more than begun in the 'secondary' stage of education! Say, if you believe it, that 'the larger meanings of life' are unimportant, but do not pretend that their study can be completed at school and therefore abandoned when we pass to the university.

It is to be hoped that we shall neither say the one nor pretend the other. It is indeed impossible and undesirable to abolish specialisation, but we can prevent it from becoming a cancer whose growth destroys studies essential to human beings as citizens and as men. Taking Professor Dewey's belief that the secondary stage in education is 'the period for the knowledge of self in relation to the larger meanings of life', we should revise it in the light of Plato's simpler and infinitely profounder words: 'The noblest of all studies is the study of what man is and of what life he should live.' We shall not agree with Professor Dewey that this 'noblest of all studies' can be completed in secondary education, but determine that in some form or another, it is indispensable in every period of education from the nursery to the grave, and see that 'the higher institution' includes it, and is not entirely reserved for 'gaining control of the particular body of knowledge and methods of research which fit the individual to apply truth to the guidance of his own special calling in life'.

So far as I know, the only universities in Britain that make definite and deliberate provision for this are the Scottish, and these do so only partially and imperfectly. Philosophy in them must be taken by all students for the *pass* degree. But this does not apply to honours students, and philosophy is generously interpreted to include such subjects as economics, and in any case may be taken in the form of logic as well as moral philosophy and metaphysics. But those who read the two latter subjects are at least confronted in their university with 'the larger meanings of life' and 'the noblest of all studies'. Outside the Scottish universities no such provision exists; and the result in some cases is, as a professor in a new university famous for its work in applied science said to me, that 'we are turning out graduates who are barbarians'. That judgment may be too severe, but there is enough truth in it to merit attention.

The real remedy is a change of heart as much as a change of curriculum, a sense of our defects and their dangers. Plato wrote over the entrance of his Academy: 'Let no one enter who is ignorant of geometry.' An admirable motto, though it might exclude some otherwise deserving scholars! But perhaps at the moment we require a rather different one to inscribe over the doors of our schools and universities. I would suggest either the words from Plato quoted on the last page, or a choice from one of the two following sayings. 'By education I mean that training in excellence from youth upwards which make a man passionately desire to be a perfect citizen, and teaches him how to rule, and to obey, with justice. This is the only education which deserves the name; the other sort of training, which aims at the acquisition of wealth or bodily strength, is not worthy to be called education at all'. 'Whatever the world thinks, he who hath not much meditated upon God, the human mind, and the *Summum Bonum*, may possibly make a thriving earthworm, but will certainly make a sorry patriot and a sorry statesman.'*

Chapter VI

EDUCATION FOR CITIZENSHIP

GREECE is the mother of education for citizenship, as of so much else. Ancient Sparta devised the most complete and ruthless discipline ever conceived for turning men into citizens and soldiers, but Athens too had her more liberal methods of civic education, and though Pericles says that she did not rely on 'rigorous training' and 'state-made courage', he claims that his countrymen 'attend both to public and private duties and do not allow absorption in their own business to interfere with knowledge of the state's affairs'. If we were asked what training in citizenship Britain gives, we might hesitate for an answer. In the last century, if the idea occurred to anyone, it interested very few: there is one reference to it in the index of an important book like Adams's *Evolution of Educational Theory* and none in Norwood's *English Tradition in England* or Nunn's *Education; its Data and First Principles*. The foundation of the Association for Education in Citizenship in 1935 is perhaps the first sign of recognition, not only that there is such a subject but that it is very important.*

Citizenship goes far beyond voting, paying taxes, sitting on a jury and the other duties expected by a nation from its members. Properly conceived, it involves all a man's actions which touch his fellow-citizens, and affect the health and well-being of the State; it is almost co-extensive with his duty to his neighbour. It includes everything which the law requires but also many duties about which it is silent and which are left to the individual conscience. It is not passive, not mere abstention from uncivic conduct. It is active. 'We regard the man who holds aloof from public duties not as "quiet" but as useless.'

'Public life is a situation of power and energy; he trespasses against his duty who sleeps upon his watch as well as he that goes over to the enemy.' The ideal state is one where every citizen is determined to be a part of the community, to share its burdens, to put its interest before his own, to sacrifice, if need be, his own wishes, convenience, time and money to it. It is a machine of which no part is idle or inefficient, none rusted, broken or ill-fitting, in which each pulley and cog takes up its full share of the load, and plays its part in the swift and smooth running of the whole. A man who evades his taxes is, so far, a bad citizen; but so is one who, in giving a vote for parliament, thinks only of his private interests, or is too indifferent or lazy to vote at all; so is the bad employer, whose treatment of his employees is not only a breach of the moral law, but adds to the social problems of the country; so are profiteers and the traders and clients of the 'black market'; so are workmen, who strike for some private interest when the existence of their country is at stake; so is the man who would be useful in local government but evades the burden, not because he cannot, but because he will not, spare the time.*

There is plenty of bad citizenship in Britain, but there is probably more good citizenship here than in any other country, though it is not always labelled by that name. It appears in the numberless gifts and legacies for charitable and kindred objects, and in the uncounted instances where private effort performs duties of public interest, ranging from the Zoological Society to the care of the blind, from the Lifeboat Institution to the Scout Movement, from the preservation of scenery and historic buildings to the work of the Motoring Associations; look through the twenty-eight pages of Societies and Institutions in *Whitaker's Almanac* if you wish to see how may national activities depend on individual enterprise. There are idle rich in Britain, but they are fewer than the less conspicuous class of wealthy or well-to-do persons, who might live wholly selfish lives but who give time and money without stint to public service. A nation where all the universities have been created by privateinititive, where municipal government and the administration of justice is largely carried on by unpaid work, where nearly half of the hospitals are managed and financed by private enterprise, where the Co-operative Movement was organised, where a third of the peace-time army is recruited by civilians giving up their leisure time to military training, where the Home Guard immediately created itself in response to public need, is not wanting in the spirit of good citizenship.

This spirit is the blood in a country's veins; where it is pure and flows strongly, national life will be healthy and vigorous, where it is thin or tainted, anaemia will be present and may pass into death. Important at any moment, it is most of all now, for we shall hardly survive the tensions of social change, certainly we shall not survive as a democracy, unless we have the community sense which will hold us together and enable us to move as a whole.

How can the spirit of citizenship be created or developed? How are good citizens made? This is part of the obscure and important question, where do men get their virtues? From what deep sources are drawn the courage and sacrifice shown in the air, by sea, on land? Where do the inhabitants of, for instance, Bermondsey or Bow, many of them living in intolerable surroundings, learn the qualities which enable them in peace to be decent, kindly people, and in war cheerfully to face the ruin of their homes and death from the air? How are such virtues to be preserved and extended? And, on the other hand, whence come our weaknesses and how shall we cure them—commercialism that sells beauty and debases standards for money, profiteering in every class and rank, partisanship and reckless statements in politics and outside it, the intellectual's betrayal of truth? Here are problems deserving inquiry more than any sociological studies, and very relevant to our future.

Citizens are made, not born; though men may be social animals, they are very apt to regard society as made for them, and as far as possible to use it for their own ends. It is an individual, not a member of a community, that issues from the womb, though these individuals have to live in the State and must learn how to do it. All human beings have the capacity to be citizens, but mere capacity is not enough; it needs developing and training. The vocational and personal sides of education will help little here. Men must learn how to earn their living; they must have the chance of developing body, mind and character to their full capacity. But earning a living and developing a personality are private matters, a concern of the individual; they will make a man a more useful member of the State but not necessarily a better citizen; they are no guarantee that he will serve it, study its interests, carry out his duties to it. Indeed if over-emphasised they may—and obviously often do—make him selfish and indifferent to the common good. Vocational and personal training are dangerously incomplete without the discipline which teaches men how to play their part in the State and makes them wish to do it. Education is a trinity, and one of its members is training in citizenship.

There are three elements in this training, of which the first and least important is teaching people the duties of a citizen and how to perform them. Mention education for citizenship, and the word 'civics' will probably rise into the mind; instruction on such subjects as 'the functions and institutions of government, both local and central, including Education, Public Health, Justice, Police, the Post Office, and the Defence Services, and the everyday work of local councils and of Parliament'.*

Eric Gill says in his *Autobiography*: 'The whole of my education was simply learning things out of little books and being able to remember enough to answer questions.' It is a common form of education. He continues: 'We are educated by the doing not by the learning and that is the whole secret of education, whether in schools or in workshops or in life.' These warnings should be remembered in considering the teaching of citizenship. At school instruction of the kind proposed is apt to be little beyond 'learning things out of little books'; at that stage there is no opportunity for 'doing'. The subject has a specious attraction, and is sometimes described as up-to-date, realistic and related to the actual needs and life of the pupil. But though apparently practical, it is in fact purely academic. It consists almost entirely in imparting facts which have no relation to the actual life of the pupil, knowledge of which he can make no immediate use. The fact that he is being educated does not mean that he will find the educational system of the country interesting; he takes no part in the work of local councils, and of parliament; and if he does not happen to be criminal, he will have no first-hand experience of either justice or the police. Unless he has a retentive memory or lively imagination, the facts learnt will fall on his mind like dust, and, like dust, will in a few months or less be swept from it by succeeding impressions, leaving perhaps a few grains of knowledge behind. The clever pupil will retain more, but is likely to derive from his studies little beyond some up-to-date knowledge of facts, a vague plausibility about social questions, and a misleading belief that he understands them. For politics and government are essentially practical subjects, wearing very different faces in books and in life. Our views on them are of small value unless we have seen them at first-hand, and a schoolboy has not seen them at first-hand.*

We must therefore not expect much from this form of instruction in citizenship. A certain amount of it is useful. In the hands of an inspired teacher, 'civics', like any other subject, can become a means of real education. But citizenship is better taught in a broader way and through the normal subjects of the school curriculum. The most fruitful part of 'civics' in the narrower sense will probably be such things as visits to town councils, law-courts, parliament, factories, a slum, a distressed area, a housing estate, etc.—when possible, abroad as well as at home. This will not impart knowledge so much as strike the imagination by a glimpse into the real thing. It is not more than a glimpse; such visits show the outside rather than the inside of problems, their existence, not their infinitely complicated conditions, but they leave in most minds a picture, a sense of real problems waiting to be solved such as all the 'little books' on civics will fail to give.*

But, it will be said, the citizen needs more than that: he ought to know something about the machinery of government and the fabric of his civilisation, and at present we fail to give him this. Certainly: but school is not the time or place to give it. It should be given when it can be used, when men and women are citizens, with votes for parliament and local government, which cannot be given effectively without knowledge and, if given effectively, can change the conditions of their life. That is the time when the knowledge is needed, is welcomed—and is not available. 'We have been told', says the report quoted above, 'that in Senior Schools, it is the citizenship lesson in which the parents show most interest and themselves provide information and send up questions for answer.' Those words indicate our neglected opportunity. Here are adults eager to learn about citizenship, unprovided with natural means to do so, and obtaining some knowledge indirectly through the lessons given to their children. But the senior school is not the best medium for teaching citizenship to men and women, nor have all adults access to it. What lovers of paradox we British are! Youth studies but cannot act; the adult must act, and has no opportunity of study; and we accept the divorce complacently. But action and thought, living and learning naturally belong together and should go hand in hand. Instruction in civics at school, if you will. But when the children are adults and have votes, let such instruction be available so that their votes can be used with intelligence. Our local government is not, in every city, the most successful of our institutions. It might be improved if every elector had an opportunity of learning something about its nature and scope, and if perhaps the newly elected City or County Councillor, instead of being thrown headlong into his duties, to learn slowly what the sea is like by swimming in it, was given some instruction in the character and variety of this vast ocean; if, in fact, we did for our municipal rulers, as much as we do for an A.R.P. Warden; for local government is as complicated and important as fire-fighting.

But this is a matter for Adult Education, hitherto so neglected in this country. At present we either fail to give our citizens the knowledge which citizens need, or push into the schools as much of it as we can manage, upsetting their curriculum and giving it at an age when it cannot be digested. We act like people who should try to give their children in a week all the food they require for a year; a method which might seem to save time and trouble, but would not improve digestion, efficiency or health. Some day, no doubt, we shall abandon this practice and give everyone a chance of thinking about life when he is facing it and about its problems when he has to solve them. When that day comes, we shall stop one of the chief sources of educational waste and inefficiency, and make the greatest advance in our history towards the creation of an educated democracy.*

But even when 'civics' is taught and taught at the right age, our task is only beginning. Knowledge of political institutions, interest in social problems and current events will not of themselves make good citizens. Pascal says, 'How far it is from the knowledge to the love of God!' We may say, 'How far it is from civics to citizenship!' We must not make the error of Socrates and think that knowledge is virtue, or that duties are performed because they are known. To study the outlines of the government of the country, to visit city councils and law courts, to have an acquaintence with economics, public affairs and current events—all this barely touches the problem. Citizenship is not information or intellectual interest, though these are part of it; it is conduct not theory, action not knowledge, and a man may be familiar with the contents of every book on the social sciences without being a good citizen.

In citizenship, as in so many provinces in life, we provide means, teach their use, but give no sense of ends; tell people how to reach the goal but leave them ignorant and doubtful of the goal itself; like persons going on a holiday, who pack their clothes, collect journey money, food, golf clubs and tennis rackets, bring the car to the door or arrange transport to the station, and then discover that they have never decided where to go. That is impossible with holidays but common with life: and training for citizenship may include 'the Monarchy and what it stands for; the Houses of Parliament and their work, to include a short history; General Elections; the Public Services—the Army, Navy, Air Force, Police, Post Office, Ministry of Labour', and much else, yet fail to give any vision of what the State should be.*

Without such a vision, the knowledge may be misused or used blindly, the means wasted for lack of the right end. Not only so, but the chief impulse to action is lost. Here, as in every sphere of life, knowledge and intellectual equipment, without an ideal to drive them, are machinery without power, and there are few more melancholy or more common sights than admirable social machinery which cannot get up enough steam to work it. The sight of an inspiring goal gives the desire to reach it, and men devise means, when they are mastered by the passion for an end. Aristotle thought that God was the source of motion in the world, not by any direct intervention but by the response of human beings to the vision of himself. 'If God is always in that good state in which we sometimes are, this compels our admiration; and if in a better state, this compels it still more. And God *is* in a better state....So he produces motion by the love he excites....On this principle depend the heavens and the world of nature.' Something of the sort is true of those visions of good which are called ideals. They have been the great sources of motion in the world, created its religious movements, made or helped its revolutions, and inspired its greatest men. Such visions 'compel our admiration and move us by the love they excite'.†

This element, small in bulk, easily and quickly imparted, yet vast in importance, must not be overlooked and forms the second element in training for citizenship. People must have a vision of the ideal State, 'the holy City, new Jerusalem, coming down from God out of heaven', that they may know the goal of their quest and desire to reach it. A bible of citizenship might well be compiled containing the great visions of the meaning of the word. It would surely contain two passages which sum up the chief articles of the creed of citizenship—duty to country and (a more neglected obligation) duty to fellow citizens. The first extract is from the speech delivered by Pericles in 431 B.C. at the public funeral of the Athenians who had fallen in the Peloponnesian war:

> Fix your eyes on the greatness of your country as you have it before you day by day, fall in love with her, and when you feel her great, remember that her greatness was won by men with courage, with knowledge of their duty, and with a sense of honour in action, who, even if they failed in some venture, would not think of depriving the country of their powers but laid them at her feet as their fairest offering.

Anyone who has listened to addresses on patriotism or tried to compose one will realise the amount of thought as well as of feeling in these few words. Patriotism is 'falling in love' with one's country (the Greek word means passionate love), and love for a country, as for a human being, springs from some supreme attraction. Men fall in love with a country because of something great in it; this greatness was created by the courage and sense of duty and unlimited self-sacrifice of individual citizens, and it inspires others to these qualities and so is maintained and extended.*

Another side of citizenship is stressed in the following passage in which it is defined as loving one's neighbour as oneself, and the State is regarded not as a mixed collection of individuals but as a united and affectionate family.

> Do not the worst evils in a state arise from anything that tends to tear it asunder and destroy its unity; and is anything better than whatever tends to bind it together and make it one? Now a state is bound together by sharing joy and sorrow, by all its citizens being equally glad or grieved on the same occasion of gain or loss. The best

ordered state will be one where the largest number of persons use the words 'mine' and 'not mine', 'another's' and 'not another's' in the same sense; it will most nearly resemble a single person. When we hurt a finger, the whole organisation of the body, unified under the ruling elements in the soul, feels it and shares the pain of the single member. The best organised community comes nearest that condition, recognises as part of itself the good and evil fortunes of each individual citizen, and shares as a whole in his joy or pain. In other states a man may regard one colleague as a friend in whom he has an interest, and another as a stranger with whom he has nothing in common. But that cannot happen with us. Our citizens must regard everyone he meets as brother or sister, father or mother, son or daughter, grandchild or grandparent. And a further point. Will you not expect them, not merely to use these family names, but to behave as a real family? In our state when things go ill or well with any of its members, everyone will use the word 'mine' in the same sense and say that all is well or ill with himself.*

Such ideals are part of a training in citizenship: they are an indication of the goal and an inspiration to reach it. But it is possible to see visions of goodness without following them, and knowledge of the right does not inevitably lead to right action. As Burke remarked:

Men are wise with but little reflection, and good with little self-denial, in the business of all times except their own. We are very uncorrupt and tolerably enlightened judges of the transactions of past ages; where no passions deceive, and where the whole train of circumstances, from the trifling cause to the tragical event, is set in an orderly series before us. Few are the partisans of departed tyranny; and to be a Whig on the business of an hundred years ago is very consistent with every advantage of present servility....Many a stern republican, after gorging himelf with a full feast of admiration of the Grecian commonwealths and of our true Saxon constitution, and discharging all the splendid bile of his virtuous indignation on King John and King James, sits down perfectly satisfied to the coarsest work and homeliest job of the day he lives in.

Bibles of citizenship—like other bibles—though guides to a

better world, are not transport to one. That journey must be done by men on their own feet, though with direction from those who best know the road.*

Here we come to the third and the most important element in training for citizenship, which we do not wholly neglect but provide sporadically and very incompletely. Citizenship, as I have urged, is practical not speculative, active not passive, an art not a theory—the art and virtue of living in a community. The good citizen, like the good soldier, has learnt to feel and act as a member of a body, to play his part in it, and, if need be, to sacrifice to it his interests and even his life, to do his duty to the State without compulsion and of his own free will. It is a difficult art, commoner perhaps in this country than in others, but not perfected, and needing to be learnt in every generation; a harmony of clashing forces—independence and respect for authority, individualism and teamwork, self-assertion, self-discipline and self-sacrifice, initiative and subordination. Knowledge of 'civics' will help men to practise it, ideals will inspire and show the goal. But Whitehead's saying that moral education is impossible without the habitual vision of greatness needs to be completed by the remark of Aristotle that men acquire virtues, not by knowing what they are nor by talking about them nor by admiring and praising them but by practising them. We become punctual by continually being punctual, we acquire the habit of telling the truth by telling it; and we become good citizens by doing what good citizens do. Social virtue is learnt by social life. So its infant school is the family, where the members, living together, learn how to live together as members of a tiny community. The smaller the family, the worse the school.

But families exist in all countries. Where have the British had the teaching which makes them not experts in the art but perhaps more expert than most peoples? I believe that much of the credit is due to religion. Foreigners recognise, even if we do not, the immense influence which Christianity has had on the national mind. Indeed, so far as we have a national mind at all, it has been mainly made by Christianity. For many hundred years most of the population of these islands heard its message preached. The conception of the Fatherhood of God, leads logically to the Brotherhood of Man; texts like 'Ye are members one of another' imply no doubt a wider citizenship than anything on earth, but they imply citizenship and enforce a sense of community. Men cannot listen to such words Sunday after Sunday without some trace of them remaining, even if it is only an ideal in the background of the mind, a pricking of the conscience, a call to the deeper side of their nature. Then too the nation has learnt much, painfully and with many failures, in a thousand years of history. It must have learnt something when Roman Catholics, Anglicans and Puritans managed to be loyal Englishmen in the days of Queen Elizabeth: more in the bitter struggles between 1640 and 1660: most of all perhaps in the admirable school of parliamentary government, where men learn to fight without becoming enemies, to lose without resentment and to win without pushing victory too far, and where the verdict of a majority is accepted but the rights of the minority are not forgotten. These are among the schools where the English have had a general social education. But there are several institutions which give it in a specific form, institutions whose members learn the habit of citizenship by being citizens. The Scout and Guide Movement, the Boys' and Church Lads' Brigades, Boys' and Girls' Clubs, are among them. Another great school of citizenship in England is the Trade Union, where several millions of Englishmen learn to subordinate private wishes and opinions to a common policy, and a mass of individuals becomes a disciplined army. A strike may be inconvenient or even unjustifiable, but men who will throw up their work and livelihood for a common cause, possibly against their desire or even their judgment, have learnt one at least of the lessons of social education—how to act as a community.*

But the greatest instrument of social education in England affects a different and much smaller though very important class. It is the so-called public school, which should rather be called the residential school. Whatever its weaknesses, it has by its very nature one great virtue. It is an incomparable school of social education, of citizenship, where boys learn citizenship by being citizens. That is what a public school boy is—a citizen. He has two countries—his school, a community of perhaps 600 boys, and his house, a community of some 50 boys. He is a member, a citizen of both these communities, and in each of them has his place and privileges and duties. He lives inside them for eight months of the year. Their problems, their interests, their happenings are before his mind on every day of those eight months. Never in later life will he be so intensely a member of a community, never again will he live so completely in and for a community, as he does in these school years. Living thus as a citizen he imbibes instinctively the fundamental principles of good citizenship. To feel yourself part of a community which you have a share and a responsibility in making, whose successes are somehow your successes and whose failures cast their shadow on you, to be able to obey and to live and co-operate with other members of the community, this is the essence of citizenship, and this the boy at a good residential school learns unconsciously every day of his life, not by being taught it, but practising it. The state no doubt is small, but there is good hope that this habit of acting as a member of a community may become part of his nature and survive when he finds himself in that larger theatre which is called a country and that still larger one which is called the world. Schools and trade unions may be narrowed to serve the interests or represent the views of a class. But this is not inherent in their nature, nor do these incidental weaknesses alter the fact that they create a spirit which may serve wider uses.

But the residential school does not provide for the masses of the nation, or for those boys who either cannot gain admission to it or whose parents prefer the day school. Where will they learn the virtues of the citizen by living as citizens?

One means is the nursery school. Plato thought that the State should educate children 'before they can understand language and are therefore incapable of appreciating any sort of instruction'; for the first 'three years are a considerable part of life to be passed ill or well'. The nursery school is based on this idea though it takes children a little later and, while the character is as little set as the body, trains them by the mere attendance at school in the art of living in a community. Nursery schools, like all institutions, have dangers but there is no reason why they should impair family life and responsibility; they supply something which the small family cannot give, and they can do much to correct the disastrous influence of bad homes.*

In the next stages the elementary school can be organised to give a practical training in citizenship, in so far as the teaching, interests and life of the school can centre in its neighbourhood. 'To be attached to the subdivision, to love the little platoon we belong to in society, is the first principle (the germ, as it were) of public affections' (Burke). At a later age the secondary day school can develop community life through school games, societies, camps and journeys abroad, etc. Here the British day school does far more for its pupils than similar institutions abroad, which limit education to the class room and consider their work done when lessons end. It is an unrecognised debt due to the residential school, from which the day school has learnt the value of extra-curricular activities, adapting them to its different circumstances. But whereas such activities are spontaneous and inevitable in the residential school, they could only be organised in the day school by the care, ingenuity and self-sacrifice of the staff, and they are one of the splendid things in British education. The good day school does everything in this direction which circumstances allow; but it can claim far less of a boy's time and life than a residential school and he is far less a citizen of it. Its weakness on this side can be seen in the newer universities, which, themselves mainly non-residential and drawing their students chiefly from non-residential schools, have in general little corporate spirit or corporate loyalty. They have done a great work in the country which must rely on them for a large part of its future leaders, but they teach rather than educate.

The following extract from *The Times* of 29 November 1937, reveals a melancholy lack of spirit of citizenship in a highly educated class of the community:

> Disappointment at the response to the—University's Extension Fund Appeal was expressed at the annual meeting of the Court of Governors to-day. The Vice-Chancellor said that 2800 copies of the Appeal had been sent to old students and only 79 had replied. It had been suggested, he continued, that old students should subscribe £1 a year for seven years, which was not an excessive amount, as most old students owed their present positions to the education they received at the university. The poor response might be partly due to the fact that students at provincial universities had become too much accustomed to receiving everything for nothing.

It is certainly surprising that, though the graduates of the university concerned had been mainly educated at public expense and largely owed their income and position to the university, there should have been so much lower a percentage of gratitude among them than among the ten lepers in the New Testament, of whom one expressed thanks for being healed. Whether such a spirit is common in other universities, I do not know.*

Whatever has been done, much remains to do. The only thorough provision, in our educational system, for training in citizenship is in the residential school—and that is unintentional. For the rest, however much the day school does, its conditions do not allow it to do as much as the nation needs, and in any case the mass of the population at present leave school at fourteen and in the future will leave it at fifteen or sixteen—ages at which training for citizenship is quite incomplete. What can we do?

The development of school camps will help; the Youth Movement has great possibilities. Still more will be done if some form of conscription or if national service persists after the war. It may take the shape of compulsory labour camps, which all members of the community must attend. They could give to the nation the training in community life which the residential school now gives to a few. They would make every Englishman 'work at least once with his hands and thus contribute towards the building up of his people. Above all, we want those who are in sedentary occupations to experience what manual labour is, so that they may feel understanding and sympathy for those of their countrymen whose lives are spent in the fields, the factory or the workshop. We want to abolish for ever that attitude of superiority which unfortunately so many of our intellectuals adopt towards the manual workers, and we wish them to realise that they too will be worth all the more if they know themselves to possess a capacity for physical work. But the ultimate aim behind labour service is to promote mutual understanding between the different classes, and thus strengthen the spirit of national solidarity among the whole people.' These are Hitler's words. But the fact that Hitler spoke them does not lessen their wisdom.*

Our first task is to realise that the spirit of citizenship does not grow into a strong plant without civilisation; our problem will be solved when everyone born in Britain has the knowledge needed by a citizen, has seen the vision of what citizenship is, and has been trained in it by living with others, not merely as an individual, but as a member of a community whose life and responsibilities he shares. I have put these three requirements in inverse order. The most important is the last.

BOOKS WRITTEN OR EDITED BY RICHARD LIVINGSTONE

Mycenae. Carmen Latinum praemio Cancellari donatum. . . (Oxford, B.H. Blackwell, 1901).

The Greek Genius and Its Meaning to Us (Oxford, Clarendon Press, 1912). Second Edition, 1915.

A Defence of Classical Education (London, Macmillan & Co., 1916).

With C. E. Freeman [eds and trans], Books IV, 20-38 and V (Books VI and VII) of *The Gallic War*, partly in the original and partly in translation. (Oxford, Clarendon Press, Clarendon Series of Latin and Greek Authors, 1919).

[ed] *The Legacy of Greece* (Oxford, Clarendon Press, 1921). A collection of essays including one by Livingstone.

[general editor] *The Clarendon Latin and Greek Series* (Oxford, Clarendon Press, 1921 ff). At first this was called the *Clarendon Series of Latin and Greek Authors*.

[ed and trans] *The Pageant of Greece* (Oxford, Clarendon Press, 1923). Selections from Greek writers in translation with biographical sketches.

[ed and trans] *The Pageant of Greece* (Oxford, Clarendon Press, 1925). Abridged edition for schools.

[ed] *The Mission of Greece. Some Greek Views of Life in the Roman World* (Oxford, Clarendon Press, 1928).

Greek Ideals and Modern Life (Oxford, Clarendon Press, 1935). Martin Classical Lectures.

'Some Thoughts on University Education' (London, Cambridge University Press, 1948). National Book League Annual Lecture No. 5.

'Leadership in Education' (London, Oxford University Press, 1950). The Walker Trust Lecture on Leadership for 1950.

Education and the Spirit of the Age (Oxford, Clarendon Press, 1952). Reprinted in 1973 by Cedric Chivers Publishers, Bath.

On Education (Cambridge, University Press, 1954). This is a combined reprint of *The Future in Education* and *Education for a World Adrift*.

'Tolerance in Theory and in Practice' (London, Council of Christians and Jews, 1954). The Robert Waley Cohen Memorial Lecture for 1954.

'Thoughts on the Education of Character' (Doncaster, Doncaster Grammar School, [1954]). The Second Vaughan Memorial Lecture.

The Rainbow Bridge and Other Essays on Education (London, Pall Mall Press, 1959). A collection of Livingstone's writings and addresses.

'The Influence of the Greek and Hebraic Traditions on Western Ideals' (London, Liberal Jewish Synagogue, [1960]). The Claude Montefiore Lecture for 1959.

'Veracity' (London, Lindsey Press, [1937]). The Essex Hall Lecture.

[ed and trans] *Portrait of Socrates. Being the Apology, Crito and Phaedo of Plato in an English Translation with Introductions and Notes*. (Oxford, Clarendon Press, 1938).

'Ends and Means' (London, University of London, 1938). This was a Birkbeck College Foundation Lecture.

[ed] *Plato: Selected Passages* (London, Oxford University Press, 1940). Oxford World Classics: no. 487. Reprinted.

The Future in Education. (Cambridge, University Press, 1941). No. 6 in the Current Problems Series, ed. by Sir Ernest Barker. Reprinted.

[ed] *Thucydides: The History of the Peloponnesian War* (London, Oxford University Press, 1943).

'Plato and Modern Education' (Cambridge, University Press, 1944). The 1944 Rede Lecture.

'Ruskin...from the Proceedings of the British Academy' (London, Oxford University Press, [1945]). Annual Lecture on a Master Mind, Henriette Hertz Trust of the British Academy.

Some Tasks for Education (London and Toronto, Oxford University Press, 1946). Lectures delivered in Canada at Victoria University and the University of Toronto.

NOTES

Unless noted otherwise all works cited were published in London.

p. v*. Quoted in *The Listener*, 1 Jan. 1942

p. v†. C.S. Lewis, *The Abolition of Man* (1978 edn., 1st publ. 1943), p. 13.

p. vi. All quotations in this Introduction from the writings of Sir Richard Livingstone are from *Education for a World Adrift* unless noted otherwise.

p. vii*. Cf. J.E.B. Munson, 'The Unionist Coalition and Eduction, 1895-1902' in *The Historical Journal* (1977).

p. viii†. *The Times*, 28 Dec. 1960. Cf. F. A. Iremonger, *William Temple Archbishop of Canterbury His Life and Letters* (1949 edn., 1st publ. 1948), p. 88 ff.

p. viii*. Alan Valentine, *The Education of an American* (1957), p. 95.

p. xii. T.S. Eliot, *Choruses from 'The Rock', 1934,* in *The Collected Poems and Plays of T.S. Eliot* (1969), stanza vi, p. 159.

p. xiv*. T.S. Eliot, *ibid.*, stanza iii, p. 155.

p. xiv†. H. H. Munro, *The Unbearable Bassington* in J.W. Lambert [ed], *The Bodley Head Saki* (1963), p. 451.

p. xv†. *The Times*, 1 May and 2 Oct. 1986; 'The Form and Manner of Ordering of Priests' in the *Book of Common Prayer*.

p. xv*. T.S. Eliot, *The Idea of a Christian Society* (1939), p. 23.

p. xviii*. Sir R.W. Livingstone [ed] (Richard Crawley [tr] revised by Richard Feetham), *Thucydides The History of the Peloponnesian War* (1943, The World Classics), p.v.

p. xviii†. H.R.H. The Prince of Wales speaking at Harvard University, Cambridge, Massachusetts, U.S.A., 4 Sept. 1986.

p. xix*. The Lord Chancellor, Lord Hailsham speaking at the British School of Archaeology, Athens, 20 June, 1986.

p. xix†. R.W. Livingstone, *The Greek Genius and Its Meaning to Us* (1912), pp. 11, 32.

p. xx. *The Times*, 28 Dec. 1960; G.L.B.O.C. [Bishop George Berkeley], *Siris: A Chain of Philosophical Reflexions and Inquiries*... (Dublin, 1744, 2nd edn, improved and corrected), §350, p. 143.

p. 3. This quote from *Hamlet*, Act I, Scene 5, should read, 'O cursed spite, That ever I was born to set it right!'

p. 4. 'Mrs Harris' is the mythical friend of Mrs Gamp, the disreputable nurse in Charles Dickens's novel, *The Life and Adventures of Martin Chuzzlewit*, published 1843-44.

The Annual Reports of the Registrars General gave a mid-year population for the United Kingdom of Great Britain and Northern Ireland in 1939 of 47,762,000. The last decennial figures, for 1931, which Sir Richard would have known, showed a population of 46,052,000 although the figure for Northern Ireland dated from 1926. There was, of course, no census taken in 1941.

Pitt made his famous remark on 9 November 1805 at the Guildhall when he was attending the Lord Mayor's banquet. He was toasted as 'The Saviour of Europe' and in reply said, 'I return you many thanks for the honour you have done me; but Europe is not to be saved by any single man. England has saved herself by her exertions, and will, I trust, save Europe by her example.' During the war, Churchill frequently quoted Pitt's reply and also wrote an introduction to a collection of his speeches.

p. 5*. There had been just such an organisation in the 19th century. The National Association for the Promotion of Social Science was established in 1857 'to collect facts, to diffuse knowledge, [and] to stimulate inquiry' in five fields: jurisprudence and amendment of the law, education, punishment and reformation, public health, and social economy. There were annual conferences and papers based on original research were read and published yearly. The Association, patterned on the British Association, was led for many years by the redoubtable Lord Brougham.

p. 5†. Aristotle, *Politics*, Book I, 2, §8. Jowett translates this as: '...the state comes into existence, originating in the bare needs of life, and continuing in existence for the sake of a good life'. (H.W.C. Davis [ed], *Aristotle's Politics translated by Benjamin Jowett*, (Oxford, Clarendon Press, 1963 edn.) p. 28.).

These lines occur in *Choruses from 'The Rock', 1934,* stanza iii.

p. 6. D. Mack Smith of All Souls College, Oxford, the acknowledged expert on Mussolini, finds this quote 'improbable' but adds, 'Mussolini said many odd things'. (D. Mack Smith to the editor, 3 Febr. 1987).

Juvenal, 10. 80, Livingstone's own translation. Throughout this book translations from the Greek and Latin may be assumed to be by Livingstone unless noted otherwise.

Plato, *Republic*, §544. Because Livingstone's translations from Plato are normally quite close to those of Benjamin Jowett, I shall also give the reference in Jowett to the passage quoted. Benjamin Jowett [tr & ed], *The Dialogues of Plato*... (Oxford, Clarendon Press, 2nd edn., 5 vols., 1875), III. 432. Hereinafter the reference will be simply Jowett, *Dialogues,* volume and page.

p. 7. In Homer's *Odyssey* Nausicaa was the daughter of King Alcinous of Phaeacia who found the shipwrecked Odysseus, fed and clothed him and brought him to her father's court.

Penelope was Odysseus's loyal wife. Although she had no word of him after the end of the Trojan war she refused to re-marry and put off her suitors by a ruse. She said she would choose one man when she had finished a tapestry on which she was working; at night she undid each day's new work and was able to fend them off until Odysseus returned after twenty years.

Cressida, in Shakespeare's play, *Troilus and Cressida*, was described by Hazlitt as 'a giddy girl, an unpractised jilt'.

Helen, who also appears in Shakespeare's play, was the wife of King Menelaus of Sparta whom she left for Paris, son of King Priam of Troy.

Portia is the loyal wife of Brutus and as such appears in Shakespeare's *Julius Caesar*. Portia is also the heroine in Shakespeare's *Merchant of Venice* in which she saves the merchant, Antonio, from Shylock's wrath.

Beatrice in this reference is presumably Shakespeare's character in *Much Ado About Nothing* although she was also Dante's guide through paradise in his *Divine Comedy*.

Thersites is speaking in Act V, scene iv of *Troilus and Cressida*. The quote should read 'What's become of the wenching rogues?...yet, in a sort, lechery eats itself.'

p. 8. Plato, *Republic,* §561. Jowett, *Dialogues*, III. 451-2.

p. 10. Cassius is speaking in Act I, scene ii of *Julius Caesar*.

F. W. Foerster, *Europe and the German Question* (London, 1941), p. 70.

St. Matthew, ch. 7, v. 14.

p. 12. Antony Ashley Cooper, 7th Earl of Shaftesbury (1801-1885), Evangelical Churchman active in a wide variety of reform movements, especially in education, sanitation, child labour and working-class housing.

John Bright (1811-1889), son of Rochdale mill owner, M.P., Quaker and famous orator for various Radical causes; advocate of *laissez faire* economics — the 'Manchester School' — and attacked Church rates, the corn laws, game-laws, capital punishment &c.

John Stuart Mill (1806-1873), Radical M.P. (1865-1868) but more famous as Utilitarian, atheist thinker and author of *On Liberty, Representative Government* and his *Autobiography*.

John Morley (1838-1923), Liberal M.P., cr. Viscount Morley. Man of letters, he edited *Fortnightly Review* and 'English Men of Letters' series; he wrote authorised biographies of W.E. Gladstone and Richard Cobden; friend of Mill and like him a self-styled 'free-thinker'.

William Ewart Gladstone (1809-1898) four times Liberal Prime Minister; although he moved from Toryism to Liberalism he retained his High Church views and was a loyal and devout Churchman.

John Henry, Cardinal Newman (1801-1890), Fellow of Oriel College, Oxford who with E.B. Pusey and John Keble started the Oxford Movement; in 1845 joined Roman Catholic church; famous for his *Apologia pro Vita Sua* and *Idea of a University*.

Benjamin Jowett (1817-1893), clergyman, Master of Balliol College, Oxford (1870-1893), luminary of Broad Church, liberal intelligentsia; translated Aristotle, Plato and Thucydides.

Thomas Carlyle (1795-1881), Scottish born writer and historian; heavily influenced by German transcendentalism which he popularised in Britain; liberal in theological views; friend of John Stuart Mill; famous for his history of the French revolution, his biography of Cromwell and his essays *Past and Present, Hero Worship* and *Chartism*.

'George Eliot' [Mary Ann Cross nee Evans] (1819-1880), regarded as novelist with 'intellectual' approach and advocate of 'free thought'; her novels include *Amos Barton, Adam Bede, Mill on the Floss, Silas Marner, Romola, Felix Holt,* and *Middlemarch.*

Matthew Arnold (1822-1888), poet and essayist; Professor of Poetry at Oxford from 1857-67; H.M.I. from 1851-1883; his most famous essays include *Culture and Anarchy, Literature and Dogma* and *Essays in Criticism.* In his analysis of English culture, with its attack on narrow provincialism ('philistinism') Arnold obviously influenced Livingstone's thought although it is not accurate to say that he 'rejected Christianity', at least not by 20th century standards.

p. 13. John Ruskin (1819-1900), writer on art, who wielded great influence in the nineteenth century. He began with criticism of art and architecture but later turned to social reform and economics in which he attacked the *laissez faire* teaching of men like Bright. His most famous works were *Seven Lamps of Architecture, Until This Last, Munera Pulveris, Sesame and Lilies* and his incomplete autobiography, *Praeterita.*

George Meredith (1828-1909), poet and novelist whose most famous book was *Diana of the Crossways.* He was awarded the O.M. in 1905.

Walter Pater (1839-1894), art critic, historian and essayist whose best known work remains *Marius the Epicurean.*

Robert Louis Stevenson (1850-1894), Scottish born novelist, essayist and poet who is today remembered for *Treasure Island, Dr Jekyll and Mr Hyde, The Child's Garden of Verse* and *Kidnapped.*

James Anthony Froude (1818-1894), historian and essayist who rejected Christianity; a close friend of Carlyle (whose literary executor he became). He is remembered for his twelve volume *History of England...* which is better as prose than as history.

George Bernard Shaw (1856-1950), Dublin-born journalist, essayist and playwright of unorthodox views; rejected Christianity for his own religion based on the 'Life Force' &c. &c. Turned against early association with socialist intellectuals like Sidney and Beatrice Webb. Won fame amongst the middle classes by attacking their 'values'.

H.G. Wells (1866-1946), novelist who specialised in 'futuristic' works and comic novels; attempted world history in *Short History of the World.*

(Enoch) Arnold Bennett (1867-1931), novelist who began with stories of his native Potteries. He then moved to novels about the provincial in the sophisticated world and on to his most famous works. *The Old Wives' Tale* and *Riceyman Steps*. Mainly remembered today for his *Clayhanger* series on life in the Potteries.

John Galsworthy (1867-1933), a novelist who explored the darker side of man's nature in his stories of middle-class English life. His most famous novels were collected in *The Forsyth Saga* and concern the acquisition of property and power. In the later volumes known as *A Modern Comedy* he shows the collapse of Victorian *mores* among the middle classes in the 1920s.

Aldous (Leonard) Huxley (1894-1963), novelist and essayist best known for *Brave New World* (1932) in which he attacks the all-powerful state which governs for the people's good; his strictures apply equally to socialism and fascism.

p. 14. This sonnet is no. 15 in *The Growth of Love* and was first published in 1876 in *XXIV Sonnets*. For Bridges see p. 55 note.

(Giles) Lytton Strachey (1880-1932), literary critic who gained notoriety in 1918 for his biographical essays, *Eminent Victorians,* which he followed with a biography of Queen Victoria in 1921. He was a practitioner of the 'debunking' school of writing and was thought clever at the time by those in revolt against 'Victorian values'.

p. 15. The parable occurs in St. Luke, ch. 11, vv. 24-26.

p. 16. Thucydides, *The History of the Peloponnesian War*, II, §37. Livingstone's translation of Pericles' famous funeral oration is based on that by Sir Alfred Zimmern which Livingstone used in his edn. of Thucydides for The World Classics published by Oxford University Press in 1943. The rest of the World Classics edn. was based on the translation by Richard Crawley (revised by Richard Feetham). cf. Livingstone [ed], *Thucydides* (1943), pp. 111-12. Zimmern's translation of Pericles' oration was first published in 1916 as *The Ideal of Citizenship; being the Speech of Pericles over Those Fallen in the War*.

p. 17*. James Bryce (1838-1922) after a highly successful career at Oxford became a don as well as an historian, barrister and Liberal M.P. from 1885 to 1896. From 1906 to 1913 he was Ambassador to the United States. One of his fields of interest was education and he was Chairman of the Royal Commission on Secondary Education. This quotation could have arisen during any of the debates on education in 1896, 1897, or 1902-3; it probably occurred during the extremely bitter debates of 1902-3. He was created Viscount Bryce in 1914. His books include, in addition to his famous history of the Holy Roman Empire, *The American Commonwealth*, and *Modern Democracies*.

p. 17†. *Charmides*, §174. Jowett, *Dialogues*, I. 35.

p. 20. Walter Lippmann, Address of 29 Dec. 1940 to the American Association for the Advancement of Science, printed in *The American Scholar* (Spring, 1941). Lippmann (1889-1974), journalist and writer, was involved in the inception of *The New Republic*, for which he wrote. He later joined the *New York World* and then, from 1931 became a columnist for the New York *Herald Tribune*. His writings were widely syndicated throughout America. Although Lippman outgrew his early socialistic leanings, he remained, like Livingstone, a liberal of the old school and was opposed to collectivism of any sort; he also insisted on the importance of morality in national life and individual development. Cf. his *A Preface to Morals* (1929).

p. 23. The School Certificate was created in the 1920s to give England and Wales for the first time one standard examination for secondary schools, administered by eight boards, to replace the variety of examinations which had existed before then. It was replaced in time by the C.S.E. and G.C.E. which are in their turn being replaced by the G.C.S.E.

p. 24. Tartarin de Tarascon is the hero of four stories by Alphonse Daudet (1840-1897) which follow the comic exploits of his hero round the world. The first, *Tartarin de Tarascon,* was published in 1872; the second, *Tartarin sur les Alpes*, in 1885; the third, *La Defense de Tarascon*, in 1886 and the fourth, *Port Tarascon* in 1890. The stories established Daudet's reputation as a writer.

Le Capitaine Pamphile was an adventure novel for children by Alexandre Dumas (père) (1802-1870), published in 1840 which featured animals in its earlier chapters and in its later chapters, a sea-captain with piratical inclinations. The first translation in English appeared in New York in 1850 and in London in 1904.

'Le Roi des Montagnes' is a short story by the French journalist and novelist, Edmond About (1828-1885), and was published in 1857.

Alexandre Dumas (père) published his most successful novel, *Le*

Comte de Monte Cristo, in 1844-1845. *Le Trois Mousquetaires* was published in 1844. His exciting tales reflected his view that the two essential ingredients in a novel, as in life, were 'l'action et l'amour'. His novels were often published in serial form in newspapers.

Johann Wolfgang Goethe (1749-1832), Romantic poet, novelist, playwright and scientist gained fame with his novel, *Die Leiden des jungen Werthers* in 1774. His great verse tragedy, *Faust,* was in two parts: the first was published in 1808 and the second in 1832, shortly after his death.

Heinrich Heine (1797-1856) the Romantic poet and writer came from a Jewish family in Dusseldorf. He lived in Paris from 1831 to his death. Although he was a novelist and writer on politics, his fame rests on his Romantic poetry.

(Johann Christoph) Friedrich Schiller (1759-1805), playwright, historian, philosopher and novelist is best remembered for his historical tragedies in verse, *Wallenstein, Maria Stuart,* and *Willhelm Tell.*

Gotthold Ephraim Lessing (1729-1781) wrote comedies, poetry, and literary criticism of the first order. He was also a philosopher (his field was aesthetics), a journalist and a writer of fables. He introduced blank verse to the German stage, wrote the first domestic tragedy and the first truly modern comedy in German.

p. 25. The account of Christ's driving devils into the Gadarene swine occurs in St. Luke, ch. 8, vv. 26-33.

p. 27. *Those who speak of the residential school as 'crushing individuality' may reflect that Sir Stafford Cripps, Mr. D.N. Pritt and Sir Oswald Mosley were all educated at Winchester.* Sir (Richard) Stafford Cripps (1889-1952), vegetarian, teetotaler and socialist, was Chancellor of the Exchequer from 1947-1950 in the Attlee administration. He is remembered for his dour intellectual appearance, his lawyer's intellect and his programme of rationing and austerity. Churchill once said of him, 'There but for the grace of God goes God.' D.N. Pritt, Q.C. (1927-1972) was a Labour M.P. from 1935 to 1950. He stood on the extreme left of the party and was chairman of various friendship committees with Eastern European communist regimes. He was awarded the Lenin Prize in 1954 and wrote a variety of pamphlets and a very long autobiography. Sir Oswald Mosley, Bart. (1896-1980) founded the British Union of Fascists in 1932. Livingstone might have added that he, too, was Wykemist.

p. 28. Ephesians, ch. 5, v. 13.

p. 29. Thucydides, *History*, II. §40, 39. Livingstone's translation is based on that by Zimmern in The Oxford World Classics edn., pp. 112-13. Pericles dominated Athens from 460 B.C. to his death in 429 B.C. He was both statesman and soldier. Under him Athens' power grew to its greatest height and the Parthenon was built.

Sir Walter Raleigh (1552?-1618), is best remembered for his adventures in the New World and against Spain but he was also an essayist, historian and poet.

William Pitt the Elder (1708-1788), cr. Earl of Chatham in 1766. One of the greatest orators in English history, Chatham dominated political life in the second half of the eighteenth century. His great love was for the classics and he urged his son, William, to read the historians Thucydides and Polybius.

Gladstone was an omnivorous reader of the classics, and of German and Italian literature, theology and 19th century British fiction. He wrote several works on Classical subjects and like Livingstone believed in the close connection of Hellenic and Christian values.

Evelyn Baring (1841-1917), cr Earl of Cromer in 1901, was a professional soldier who became one of the greatest of Imperial administrators. His fame rests on his many reforms in Egypt aimed at improving the quality of life for the masses but he was also an essayist and historian. His works included *Modern Egypt* and *Ancient and Modern Imperialism*.

General James Wolfe (1727-1759), gained Canada for the Crown when he led his troops at night down the St Lawrence to scale the heights above Quebec; he was killed on the Plains of Abraham in the battle which ensued. According to a young midshipman who was in Wolfe's boat on the St Lawrence, Wolfe, with a low voice, recited Gray's *Elegy in a Country Churchyard* to the officers round him, perhaps to relieve the strain. 'Gentleman' he said, after he had finished, 'I would rather have written those lines than take Quebec.' Thomas Gray (1716-1771) had finished the poem in 1750, nine years before and legend has it that it was Wolfe's fiancée who had given him his copy of the poem.

Charles James Fox (1749-1806), is remembered as the leader of the

Whig party from 1782 to 1806 and as a rake but he also enjoyed literature and wrote a history of the Whig revolution of 1688 which was published after his death. He would have read Euripides' 5th century B.C. plays in the original Greek.

The best record of Caesar's experiences during the Gallic wars remains his own history, *De Bello Gallico* , more properly known as his *Commentarii.* The work shows him to have been not only a great general but a good historian.

Menander (c. 342-292 B.C.) was an Athenian dramatist whose plays were known for their realistic treatment of contemporary life.

p. 30. The Arnold referred to here is not Matthew Arnold but his father, the Rev Thomas Arnold (1795-1842), who, as Headmaster of Rugby from 1828 to 1842, modernised the curriculum by adding modern history, languages and mathematics to the Classics.

p. 33*. *I do not mean to put the two visions — modern Germany and modern Russia — on a level.* Sir Richard, like many others during the War, was ignorant of the true extent of Stalin's atrocities against his own countrymen, especially Ukrainians, Christians, intellectuals, small farmers and even fellow communists: his evil deeds even exceeded those of Hitler in the number and extent of his victims.

p. 33†. *The Aims of Education and Other Essays* (London, 1929), p. 106. Alfred North Whitehead (1861-1947) was born in England and educated at Cambridge. He was Professor of Applied Mathematics at London's Imperial College from 1911-1924; he was Professor of Philosophy at Harvard from 1924 to 1936. His early fame rested as much on his mathematical work as on his philosophy.

p. 36. *Phaedrus*, §247. Jowett, *Dialogues*, II. 124. The complete quote in Jowett is, 'The divine intelligence, nurtured upon mind and pure knowledge, and the intelligence of every soul which is capable of receiving the food proper to it, rejoices at beholding Reality, and once more gazing upon Truth, is replenished and made glad, until the revolution of the worlds brings her round again to the same place.'

p. 38. Plato, *Protagoras*, §325-6. Jowett, *Dialogues,* I. 138-9.

p. 40. Montaigne, *Essais*, I. 25. Livingstone's own translation. The quote is actually found not in Essay 25 but in Essay 26, 'Of the

Education of Boys'. In Trechmann's translation the sentence quoted reads, 'But let my tutor remember the object of his charge and impress upon his pupil not so much the date of the ruin of Carthage as the character of Hannibal and Scipio, not so much where Marcellus died as why it was unworthy of his duty to die there.' In Essay 25 Montaigne also wrote, 'We should enquire who knows best, not who knows most.' (E.J. Trechmann [tr], *The Essays of Montaigne* (London, two vols., 1927), I. 155, 133. The first two books of *Essais* by Michel Eyquem de Montaigne (1533-1592) appeared in 1580; in 1588 a third was published along with the first two.

Hannibal (247-183/2 B.C.) was the Carthaginian general who still ranks as one of the world's greatest soldiers. He was a superb tactician and leader. He precipitated the Second Punic War by attacking Rome's ally, Saguntum, in Spain. He is remembered today for his feat in 218 B.C. when he led an army of 30,000 over the Alps in a pre-emptive move into Italy. Although he campaigned there successfully for 16 years he never took Rome and was recalled to Africa where he was defeated in 202 B.C. He escaped to Carthage where he urged peace and left soldiering for politics. He eventually committed suicide in Bithynia to avoid being extradicted to Rome.

Publius Cornelius Scipio Africanus Major (236 or 235 — c 183 B.C.) was the Roman general who conquered Spain and defeated Hannibal in 202 B.C. at the battle of Zama. He was famed as an upright man and when charged with embezzlement in 185 B.C. he reminded his accusers that the day marked the anniversary of the battle and spurned the charge.

p. 41 Quintus Septimius Florens Tertullian (c 160-220) was one of the most important of the Church's Early Fathers. He was a native of Carthage and was trained as a lawyer; his legal training gave his writing a precision that has been a characteristic of western theology. His private life was marked by a severe asceticism which traced its origin to the Montanist movement of the 2nd century, a movement which was also apocalyptic. It is to these aspects of Tertullian's character that Livingstone is referring.

Michael Faraday (1791-1867) in 1831 discovered magneto-electricity and was responsible for other scientific discoveries. In his religious beliefs Faraday was a Sandemanian, i.e. a follower of the sect established by the Scottish minister, John Glas, which rejected an established church, preached the sole efficiacy of faith alone, practised foot-washing and celebrated the *agape* with broth.

Charles (Robert) Darwin (1809-1882) gained fame in 1859 when he published his *Origin of Species* setting forth his theory of natural evolution; his *Descent of Man* was published in 1871.

Louis Pasteur (1822-1895), the French chemist and biologist, established the modern science of bacteriology and did much to forward preventive medicine; he discovered a method to inoculate for hydrophobia.

Adam Smith (1723-1790), economist and philosopher whose book, *The Wealth of Nations,* published in 1776, began the study of political economy as a separate academic discipline.

Socrates (469-399 B.C.), although regarded as one of the founders of Greek philosophy, wrote nothing; his influence was seen in Plato's various dialogues. Broadly speaking his teaching was (1) the need to investigate all aspects of knowledge, belief and behaviour and (2) that knowledge is necessary for virtue and therefore wickedness comes from ignorance. His 'method' was that by putting a number of questions, each referring to the previous answer, one could arrive at a precise answer to the question first posed, the 'Socratic method'.

Plato (c. 427-348 B.C.) was a pupil of Socrates whose methods he adopted as seen in his Dialogues, e.g. *Republic, Laws, Symposium* and *Protagoras*. In the fields of ethics and epistomology he developed the theory of the Idea, the absolute and eternal *form* of an object or value which man can know and which alone can act as the standard for understanding life on earth.

The Stoics were a school of Greek philosophy founded by Zeno in the early 4th century B.C. which taught that man's well being lies in being freed of the passions so as to approximate God's will. Such self-control makes virtue possible; suffering therefore is irrelevant. Among its most famous advocates were Senecca and Marcus Aurelius.

St Augustine of Hippo (345-430), the greatest of the Doctors of the Church, stands among her greatest theologians. He did much to defend orthodox Christianity against contemporary heresies and it is ironic, therefore, that his writings inspired Luther in the 16th century. His most famous works are *Confessions* and *The City of God*.

St Thomas Aquinas (c. 1225-1274) is remembered for his role in the 'mediaeval' or 'scholastic' theology of the church by his insistence on reconciling the newly discovered writings of Greece and Rome with Christianity. His massive *Summa Theologica*, influenced by his study of Aristotle, remains a monument of European thought.

Alexander the Great (356-323 B.C.) was the son of Philip II of Macedon and was taught by Aristotle; he led Greek armies against Persia which he conquered; his empire extended into Egypt and India. He founded the city of Alexandria in the Nile delta.

Gaius Julius Caesar Octavianus [Augustine] (63 B.C.-A.D. 14) was the nephew of Julius Caesar and the first Roman Emperor, from 27 B.C. till his death. The title 'augustus' was conferred on him when he became emperor.

Charlemagne [Charles the Great] (742-814) was King of the Franks whose empire extended into modern-day Germany and Spain; in 800 he was proclaimed Holy Roman Emperor when the Pope re-created the Roman Empire in Western Europe. In addition to his military achievements he is famed for his patronage of learning and writing and for his civil, judicial and ecclesiastical reforms.

Nick Bottom, speaking in *A Midsummer-Night's Dream*, Act I, scene 1.

p. 42. The philosopher, Democritus, was born c. 460 B.C. and wrote about the natural sciences, music and mathematics as well as ethics. He propounded the theory that the material world was made up of a concourse of atoms; he was nicknamed the 'laughing philosopher' for his enjoyment of man's follies.

St Bernard of Clairvaux (1090-1153) was the greatest member of the newly founded Cistercian Order of monks; his saintly character, his mysticism, sermons and writings made him a great force in his day and helped the new order to grow.

John of Salisbury (c. 1115-1180), after studying in France and serving in the papal service, returned to England and was secretary to St Thomas à Becket whom he supported against Henry II. In 1176 he became Bishop of Chartres which he remained until his death. He was a man of letters and a philosopher and he was the first European to become fully acquained with Aristotle's *Organon* — the body of his writings on logic.

Henry I (1068-1135) usurped the English Throne from his older brother, Robert, on the death of their brother, William II, thereby becoming the third Norman King of England. A crafty ruler, he married Matilda, daughter of Malcolm III of Scotland whose mother had been St Margaret and whose grandfather, Duncan I, had been killed by Macbeth. Henry I did much to organise the judicial system by sending out High Court judges on circuit; he also built up his Anglo-Norman possessions. He was buried at Reading Abbey.

Frederick I [Barbarossa] (c. 1123-1190) became Holy Roman Emperor in 1152 with the desire to build up a united Germany and a strong throne against the papacy's power. To weaken Rome he tried to gain control of northern Italy and in 1160 he repudited the Pope by recognising the anti-pope, Victor IV. His power in Germany now weakened, he led the Third Crusade to recover Jerusalem from the Mohammedans and he died while on crusade. His nick-name refers to his red beard. The Nazi Party made a great cult of him.

St Thomas More (1478-1535) became Lord Chancellor in 1529 on the fall of Cardinal Wolsey. Although a reformer, like his friend Erasmus, he could not accept Parliament's claim, on the tyrant, Henry VIII's orders, to be able to sever the Church in England from Rome and he therefore retired from public life so as not to have to refuse to subscribe to Henry VIII's Act of Supremacy. He was beheaded on 6 July 1535 and was canonized 400 years laters by Pope Pius VI.

Nicholas Copernicus (1473-1543) is widely regarded as the father of modern astronomy with his theory that the sun, not the earth, was the centre of the solar system. This helped man to understand the progression of the seasons, the movement of the stars and the nature of the equinoxes.

For Lord Shaftesbury see p. 12 n. 1.

Prince Otto von Bismarck (1815-1898), the architect of the German Empire (1871-1918). As Prime Minister of the King of Prussia his goal was to make Prussia dominate Germany through a second *reich* or empire of which the Prussian King would be Emperor. He became the new empire's first 'chancellor' or Prime Minister. A flatulent and obnoxious Prussian militarist, he stamped his character on the Empire he shaped; he finally lost power in 1890.

Camillo Benso, Count di Cavour (1810-1861), was twice Prime Minister to the King of Sardinia; his goal was to build up the House of Savoy and to unite the various Italian nations under the Sardinian throne at the expense of the Pope, the Austrian Emperor and the various other ruling houses. This was largely done by the time of his death and like Bismarck he is regarded as the unifier of his nation.

p. 43*. Hosea, ch. 6, v. 6 reads: 'For I desired mercy, and not sacrifice; and the knowledge of God more than burnt offerings.'

St Matthew, ch. 5, vv. 43-45 read: 'Ye have heard that it hath been said, Thou shalt love thy neighbour, and hate thine enemy. But I say unto you, Love your enemies, bless them that curse you, do good to them that hate you, and pray for them which despitefully use you, and persecute you; That ye may be the children of your Father which is in heaven: for he maketh his sun to rise on the evil and on the good, and sendeth rain on the just and on the unjust.'

p. 43†. *There is a good life by James Cotter Morison,* The Life and Times of St Bernard *(London, 1863).*

The lines beginning 'Their shoulders held...' are found in A. E. Housman's poem, 'Epitaph on an Army of Mercenaries' and should read:

Their shoulders held the sky suspended;
  They stood, and earth's foundations stay;
What God abandoned, these defended,
  And saved the sum of things for pay.

p. 44. Arnold's poem, 'Morality' was first published in 1852 and was meant by him to supplement his poem, 'Self-Dependence'.

The couplet, 'When love is an unerring light/And joy its own security', occurs in the third stanza of Wordsworth's 'Ode to Duty' written in 1805. It appeared in 1807 in *Poems in Two Volumes.*

'The Character of the Happy Warrior' was composed in December 1805/January 1806 and was first published in 1807.

'The Prelude', although finished in 1805, was not published until after Wordsworth's death in 1850.

Benedict (Baruch) de Spinoza (1632-1677), the philosopher, was a Jew of Portuguese origin born at Amsterdam although he was expelled the synagogue because of his criticism of the Scriptures. His most famous work is his *Ethics*, which he finished about 1665 although it was not published until 1677. To Spinoza, God was the immanent cause of the universe, not its ruler.

Immanuel Kant (1724-1804) taught in the East Prussian University of Königsberg, now Kaliningrad in Poland. Kant's various philosophical works, especially those on ethics and epistomology, have had considerable influence, notably on the German philosophers Fichte, Schelling and Hegel.

p. 45*. Sir Richard confused the character of the leech-gatherer with the poem in which he occurs, i.e. 'Resolution and Independence' which was composed in 1802 and first published in 1807. The old leech-gatherer appears in stanza viii. The quote attributed to the leech-gatherer, beginning 'In common things...' does not appear in 'Resolution and Independence' but in verse xiii of Wordsworth's poem, 'A Poet's Epitaph', composed in 1799 and published in 1800.

p. 45†. The first three books of *The Faerie Queen* by Edmund Spenser (1552?-1599) were published in 1589, the second three, in 1596.

John Milton (1608-1674), the greatest product of English puritanism, wrote his massive epic, *Paradise Lost*, after he had lost his position in the Commonwealth with the collapse of Cromwell's dictatorship and the Restoration of constitutional government under Charles II in 1660. According to John Aubrey the poem was finished in 1663.

Percy Bysshe Shelley (1792-1822) published his four act lyrical drama, *Prometheus Unbound,* in 1820. In the drama, Prometheus is portrayed as the champion of mankind fighting against the seemingly omnipotent power of Jupiter.

Alfred Tennyson (1809-1892) published 'The Morte d' Arthur' in 1842; it became the first instalment of what was to become one of his greatest works, *The Idylls of the King*. Other poems drawing on the Arthurian legends continued to appear seriatim over the next forty years and together make up the *Idylls*.

p. 46. R.W. Church, *Spenser* (London, 1879, English Men of letters Series), p. 151. R. W. Church (1815-1890) was Dean of St Paul's Cathedral from 1871-1890; he had been a close friend of Newman's and was a leading member and historian of the Oxford movement.

p. 47. In *Hamlet* it was Claudius who murdered his brother, the King, and then married his widow, Hamlet's mother, whom he had already seduced.

In *Cymbeline*, Iachimo, spurned by Imogen, gains entry into her chamber and obtains evidence to trick her husband, Leonatus Posthumus, into thinking she has been unfaithful.

In *Othello* the jealous Iago takes his revenge on Othello by convincing him that Desdemona, his wife, has been unfaithful; Othello in his turn murders Desdemona in a fit of jealous rage.

In *Hamlet*, Horatio is Hamlet's loyal friend.

In *Cymbeline*, Imogen is the falsely accused but loyal wife.

In *King Lear*, Cordelia is Lear's youngest daughter and the only one loyal to him and it is Cordelia who receives her father when he is brought to her as a blind mad-man. In the same play it is the Earl of Kent who is the faithful friend of King Lear.

In *Hamlet* Polonius is the loquatious but harmless Lord Chamberlain, a well-meaning and honourable character if slightly humourous. Osric is a courtier who brings the message to Hamlet that Claudius has arranged a duel between Hamlet and Laertes.

In *The Winter's Tale*, it is Paulina who tries in vain to reconcile Leonates and his estranged wife, Hermione. Later in the play she accomplishes her aim.

In *King Lear*, the Earl of Gloucester takes pity on Lear and is blinded by the Duke of Cornwall, husband of one of Lear's two wicked daughters (Regan). Edmund is a bastard son of the Earl of Gloucester who sides with Lear's rebellious daughters; he eventually has Cordelia and her father imprisoned, and Cordelia hanged. In time he is ousted from power.

William Wycherley (1640-1716), the Restoration playwright and poet, had in the 19th century a reputation for vulgarity and indecency, and this is the view held by Livingstone. In our own century he is regarded more as a superb satirist.

Dun Juan by Lord Byron was published 1819-1824 and was unfinished. The poem has been described as a social comedy and satire but to the Victorians it was decidedly naughty.

p. 48*. The tares occur in Christ's parable of the sower in St Matthew, ch. 13, vv. 24-30.

Attila the Hun, who died in 453, was the 5th century terror of Europe. His raids went as far south as Rome and he only desisted at his attempts to capture the city when beseeched by Pope Leo I. He became known as the *flagellum Dei*, the scourge of God.

Cesare Borgia (1475-1507) was the son of Pope Alexander VI and became Captain General of the Church. He led the papal armies and became known for his unscrupulous and merciless manner. He is said to have been the original for Machiavelli's prince in *Il Principe*.

Armand Jean du Plesis, Cardinal Richelieu (1585-1642) was a Bishop who became in effect ruler of France under Louis XIII in

1629. To Englishmen he has always been associated with the persecution of French Protestants.

Frederick II — the Great (1712-1786) was King of Prussia after 1740. Although he was a gifted musician, a skilled translator and in some ways an enlightened ruler, he is remembered for his military prowress and his despotic ways.

François Villon (b. 1431) was a French poet and scholar of the Sorbonne who described his riotous career, including his near escape from execution for theft, in his *Petit Testament, Grand Testament* and ballads.

Giovanni Boccaccio (1313-1375) was a Florentine diplomat, humanist, poet and biographer of Dante. He is best remembered for his collection of tales in *The Decameron* in which ten people fleeing the Black Death in Florence each tell ten stories during their ten day trip. His work, known for its earthiness, influenced, among others, Chaucer and Shakespeare.

The Restoration Dramatists, notably Wycherley, Congreve, Farquhar and Vanbrugh flourished in the period after the Restoration of Charles II in 1660. Their work was marked by ribald humour, a sardonic approach and cynicism.

Thomas, Cardinal Wolsey (1475?-1530) was Henry VIII's Lord Chancellor from 1515 to 1529. He was a notorious pluralist and tried to arrange the King's divorce from Queen Katherine. He fell from power partly due to the dislike of Anne Boleyn and died while on his return to London to face a contrived charge of high treason.

Stendhal, pseudonym of Henri Beyle (1783-1842), French novelist, essayist and journalist. After the restoration of Louis XVIII 'Stendhal', a Bonapartist, went to Italy. His greatest novels were *Le Rouge et le Noir* (1830) and *La Chartreuse de Parme* (1839).

George Gordon, 6th Baron Byron (1788-1824), the much idealised Romantic poet. A profligate to Victorians, his private life would today be the common coin of television chat-shows. To the Duke of Wellington, Byron was 'a rum fellow'.

St Augustine of Hippo [Charles Brigg, ed & trans.], *Confessions* (London, 1893), I. 16, II. 10. Livingstone based his translation on that of Brigg.

p. 48†. The phrase 'natural end of man...' was used by T. S. Eliot but the editor is unable to trace its source.

Plato, *Republic*, §377. This translation is taken from F.N. Cornford [trans & ed], *The Republic of Plato* (Oxford, Clarendon Press, 1941), p. 67.

p. 49. Jacob, son of Isaac and grandson of Abraham, got his twin brother, Esau, to give him his birthright in exchange for a mess of pottage. Jacob went on to impersonate his brother and gain Isaac's death-bed blessing. His name means 'supplanter' in Hebrew. [Genesis, ch. 25, vv. 24-34].

Jael was the wife of Heber the Kenite who gave refuge to Sisera, captain of the forces of the King of Canaan and sent to put down an uprising by the Jews whom the king had enslaved. Sisera had been defeated and was fleeing for his life. Jael's husband, although a Jew, was not part of the uprising. After welcoming Sisera, giving him milk and agreeing to hide him she drove a tent peg through his skull as he slept, pinning him to the ground. The Old Testament writer, or perhaps the translator, in a masterful understatement, added 'So he died.' [Judges, ch. 4, vv. 1-23].

It has, however, been done admirably for the Psalms in R.B. Henderson [ed], The School Liturgy Prayers, Psalms and Hymns for Use in Schools *(London, rev. edn., [1922])*.

Oscar Wilde's quip was occasioned when he reportedly heard that a fellow poet, John Barlas, was said to have gone mad as a result of reading the Bible. See Francis Gribble, 'Magdalen College' in *The Romance of the Oxford Colleges* (London, 1910), pp. 164-70.

Samuel's bloody order to Saul appears in I Samuel, ch. 15, v. 3.

Cf the picture of the Covenanters in Sir Walter Scott's novel, Old Mortality. The novel was published in 1816. One could also cite the 'Fundamentalists' in America.

p. 50. St Matthew, ch. 6, v. 23.

Abraham Lincoln (1809-1865), 16th President of the United States is no longer universally recognised as a 'great man' in the sense Livingstone meant. His election caused the secession of thirteen Southern states to form the Confederate States of America. Lincoln is seen today as a wily politician; his despotic use of power along with his fraudulent second election in 1864 exposed his moral posturing, as in his Second Inaugural Address in March, 1865 for what it was. He was assassinated on Good Friday, 1865, while attending the theatre.

p. 51. Thomas Garrigue Masaryk (1850-1937), born in Moravia in the Austrian Empire, was apprenticed to a blacksmith; through his mother's determination he got an education and became a teacher and eventually a lecturer in philosophy in the University of Vienna; he then became a professor in the new Czech University of Prague. He entered the Imperial Parliament in Vienna as a Czech nationalist, opposing the Empire's foreign policy, especially in Bosnia. He fled when war broke out in 1914 and worked in various Allied nations against Austria and for an independent nation of Czechs and Slovaks. In 1917 he got the Americans to support his plan for a dismemberment of the Empire and he became the first President of Czechoslovakia in 1918 and was re-elected in 1920 and 1927. His son, Jan, became a diplomat in the new Republic and saw its inevitable absorption in the new, Communist Empire which filled the vacuum created by his father's anti-Austrian policy. The communists claimed he had committed suicide by defenestration in 1948 in Prague.

Lord Acton, 'The Study of History' in J.N. Figgis & R.V. Laurence (eds), *Lectures on Modern History* (London, 1926 edn), pp. 24,25. Sir John Emerich Edward Dalberg-Acton, 8th baronet and 1st Baron Acton (1834-1902) came from a Roman Catholic family and was possessed of a vast erudition. He was a Whig M.P. from 1859-1865 and a liberal-minded Catholic who opposed, but finally accepted, the decree of Papal Infallibility of 1870. He amassed a library of 50,000 volumes which was bought for Cambridge after his death. He helped to found the *English Historical Review* and was Regius Professor of Modern History at Cambridge from 1895 till his death. 'The Study of History' was his inaugural lecture delivered at Cambridge on 11 June 1895. He planned the *Cambridge Modern History*. After his death were published, in addition to *Lectures on Modern History, The History of Freedom, Historical Essays and Studies* and *Lectures on the French Revolution.*

p. 52. John Henry, Cardinal Newman, *The Scope and Nature of University Education* (London, Everyman's Library, 1965 edn), pp 199-200. Newman's lectures were given before the Catholic University of Dublin in 1852.

p. 53. Newman, *Scope and Nature...*, pp. 202-3.

p. 54*. Aeschylus (525-456 B.C.) is regarded as the founder of Greek tragedy because he introduced a second actor where before there had only been one actor and the chorus and because he subordinated the chorus to the dialogue.

p. 54†. Alfred Edward Housman (1859-1936) was Professor of Latin at Cambridge and a noted classical scholar although his fame rests on his lyric verse, *A Shropshire Lad* (1896) and *Last Poems* (1922).

(William) Somerset Maugham (1874-1965) wrote not only novels but plays and short stories. His fame largely rests on his novels, especially *Of Human Bondage* (1915), *The Moon and Sixpence* (1919) and *Cakes and Ales* (1930).

James (Augustine Aloysius) Joyce (1882-1941), Dublin-born novelist beloved of literary critics and intellectuals. His most famous works, such as *Ulysses* (1922) and *Finnegans Wake* (1939) made great use of the 'stream of consciousness' device. His other famous book, *A Portrait of the Artist as a Young man* (1914-1915), is autobiographical. He also wrote plays and short stories.

p. 55*. The Book of Isaiah contains the prophet's messianic visions and prophecies and contains some of the most beautiful and well known verses in the Old Testament.

The *Book of Judges*, on the other hand, is the 7th book of the Old Testament, and traces the history of the Jews from Joshua's death to the establishment of the monarchy. It describes the bloody conquest of Palestine under a succession of leaders or 'judges' until the time of Saul. *The Book of the Prophet Isaiah*, stresses the need for man to offer spiritual worship as well as sacrifice to God and points to the Messiah who will save mankind.

Virgil (70-19 B.C.) is remembered by every schoolboy as author of the epic, *The Aeneid.* Virgil has been honoured throughout Christian history as an *anima naturaliter Christiana* (naturally Christian soul) because of his high moral tone in the *Aeneid* and because of the messianic aspect of his Fourth Eclogue. In the Divine Comedy, it was Virgil who was Dante's guide through hell and purgatory.

Publius Ovidius Naso or Ovid (43 B.C.-A.D. 18) on the other hand, was not only famous for his Latin elegiacs but for personal scandal and amorous verses; he was exiled by Augustus in A.D. 8.

Christopher Marlowe (1564-1593) was famous not only for his *Tragedy of Dr Faustus, Jew of Malta* and *Edward II* but for the scandals of his short private life. He was reputed to have been a secret government agent and was notorious for his atheism.

For John Milton see p. 45† note.

William Congreve (1670-1729) gained fame for his skill in writing the 'comedy of manners' including *The Way of the World, The Double Dealer* and *Love for Love*. Although now popular again for his wit and repartee in dialogue he was shunned for his profanity and licentiousness. If Milton is 'sacred', Congreve is 'profane'.

Samuel Johnson (1709-1784) is best remembered today for his *Dictionary*, begun in 1747 and for his conversation, recorded by James Boswell in his *Life*, published in 1791. In his time he ranked as England's greatest man of letters, as an essayist, scholar, editor and critic. His private life was marked by nobility of character and devotion to the Church of England.

Laurence Sterne (1713-1768), although a clergyman, felt more at home in the literary circles of London than in his Yorkshire parish. His novels, the most famous of which remains *Tristram Shandy* (1760-1767), were sometimes marked by a vulgarity which even 18th century readers found excessive. He died alone and a pauper.

Percy Bysshe Shelley (1792-1822), although his married life was scandalous, was marked as a man by gentleness, loyalty and generosity, e.g. in his relations with Leigh Hunt. These attributes cannot be said to have applied in equal measure to Byron.

George Moore (1853-1933), the Irish poet, playwright, short story writer, novelist and critic, published his first collection of poems, *Flowers of Passion* in 1878, followed by *Pagan Poetry* in 1882. His novels were greatly influenced in their realism by French writers such as Zola, Flaubert and Balzac. He entertained a hatred for Christianity, especially the Roman Catholic Church. Meredith's work, on the other hand, while marked by a capacity for character analysis had a strong optimism which allowed him to triumph over the darker sides of man's existence.

Robert Bridges (1844-1930) trained as a physician but gave up medicine for writing in 1882. His greatest work as a poet came between 1885 and 1916. In 1913 he was appointed Poet Laureate. His lyrical poetry was marked by subtlety and restraint. He also wrote short stories and plays. He was interested in church music and wrote one oratorio. A.E. Housman, however, held quite unorthodox religious views.

This may be translated as 'That which is always held, everywhere and by everyone as opposed to that which is held sometimes, in some places and by some people.' Livingstone's rule 'quod semper...' is an adaptation of what is known as the Vincentian Canon. This was devised by St Vincent of Lerins in his *Commonitorium* (II.3) in the 5th century as a test of true as opposed to false tradition and read 'quod ubique, quod semper, quod ab omnibus creditum est' — 'that which has been believed everywhere, always and by everyone'.

p. 55† The *Index Expurgatorius* was the list of passages to be removed or re-written in specified books which could otherwise not be read by Roman Catholics. The criteria for the *Index* was first drawn up by the Council of Trent. It should not be confused with the *Index Librorum Prohibitorum* which was the list of books forbidden to the faithful. Both indices were abolished under Pope Paul VI in 1966.

p. 56. Edward FitzGerald (1809-1883) lived a retired life in Suffolk although he was a friend of many great Victorian writers including Tennyson, Thackeray and Carlyle. He published many translations from the Greek but is remembered for his 1859 free translation from the Persian of the *Rubaiyat of Omar Khayyam* published anonymously. His version eventually gained him considerable fame and influence.

p. 57*. William Empson, speaking on the B.B.C. Overseas Service and quoted in 'Did You Hear That?' in *The Listener*, 1 Jan 1942. Empson had been a Lecturer for several years at Tokyo University. He also wrote an article on Japan which was published in *The Listener* on 5 March 1942.

p. 57†. The quote on 'sexual respectability' comes from George Sampson, *The Concise Cambridge History of English Literature* (Cambridge, 1941), p. 504.

Robert Burns (1759-1796) was famous not just for his poetry, satire and songs but for his loose living which in time undermined his health.

p. 59. Plato [Cornford, tr], *The Republic*, p. 88.

p. 60. Plato, *Laws,* §653. Jowett, *Dialogues*, V. 222.

p. 61. Plato, *Meno,* §98. Jowett, *Dialogues,* I. 302.

T.S. Eliot, *Selected Essays 1917-1932* (London, 1st edn, 1932), p. 384.

p. 64. Dante Alighieri [Robert Laurence Binyon tr], *Inferno* (London, 1933), XXVI. 118.

Richard Foxe (1448?-1528) was successively Bishop of Exeter, Bath and Wells, Durham, and Winchester; his real work was as a diplomat for Henry VII. Under Henry VIII he was supplanted by Wolsey and he then turned to his episcopal duties. He supported the 'new learning' along with More and Erasmus and the foundation of Corpus Christi College was evidence of this.

The Greek *areté* can be translated as 'virtue', that is the function for which an object or being, including man, is designed and in which it — or he — is fulfilled; the Greek *episteme* means knowledge, cf 'epistomology', the philosophical study of the means and foundation of man's knowing.

p. 65*. Sir Richard's translation is based on that by Cornford (*The Republic,* §444, p. 140) which reads, 'It appears, then, that virtue is as it were the health and comeliness and well-being of the soul, as wickedness is disease, deformity, and weakness.'

p. 65†. T.H. Green [A.C. Bradley ed], *Prolegomena to Ethics* (London 1883), §249 f. Thomas Hill Green (1836-1882) was a tutor and Fellow of Balliol College, Oxford; from 1878 he was Whyte Professor of Moral Philosophy at Oxford. He was a follower of Kant and Hegel and propagated their work in English-speaking countries.

p. 68*. For a further account of *areté* cf R.W. Livingstone, *Greek Ideals and Modern Life* (Oxford, Clarendon Press, 1935), p. 69 f.

p. 68†. Epictetus (c. 50-c. 130) had been a slave and rose to become one of the most famous Stoic teachers and philosophers in the Roman Empire; in certain aspects his concept of God resembles Christianity.

Marcus Aurelius (121-180) was Roman Emperor from 161 and is one of the most famous Stoics. He stood apart from both Christianity and the official paganism of the Roman Empire. He wrote down his own 'thoughts' or *Meditations* which have been widely read in the centuries following his death.

A.N. Whitehead, *Adventures of Ideas* (Cambridge, 1933), p. 15. *There is no more stimulating and instructive book on Western civilisation.*

p. 68††. *Vide* Harris Rackham [trans), *Aristotle's Ethics for English Readers* (London, 1943). This was in preparation while Sir Richard was writing. Rackham's 1932 translation of *The Politics* by Aristotle (in the Loeb Classical Library) was praised by Livingstone. It was republished in 1959 and 1972.

Books III. c. 6 to IV fin. These books and X. 6 to end are of most interest to the ordinary reader.

p. 69. *For Socrates and Plato, the World's Classics* Selections from Plato, The Republic, *translated and edited by Professor Cornford*, Portrait of Socrates, *by Sir R. W. Livingstone: for the Stoics, any good translation of Epictetus such as that in Oxford Classical Translations, and Marcus Aurelius in the same series. The above books on Plato recommended because they have an introduction and notes for English readers; reading translations of Plato which give no such guidance is apt to be unprofitable.*

p. 70. Jesus used the phrase, 'the abomination of desolation' in St Matthew, ch. 24, v. 15 when speaking of the signs indicating the end of the world. He was referring to Daniel's instruction by the angel Gabriel (in Daniel, ch. 9, vv. 21-27) concerning the pollution of the Temple in Jerusalem. (Cf Daniel, ch. 11, v. 31 and ch. 12, v. 11).

The quotation is from Matthew Arnold's poem, 'The Scholar Gipsy', published in 1853 and should read 'Vague half-believers of our casual creeds'.

R.W. Livingstone, *The Future in Education* (Cambridge, 1941), pp. 125-6. This was the 6th volume in Cambridge University Press's series, Current Problems, edited by Sir Ernest Barker. [The quote from St John's Gospel is found in ch. 20, v. 31.]

p. 71. *Probably the early Christian recited the Creed only once in his life, at his Baptism.*

Plato, *Laws*, §659. Jowett, *Dialogues*, V. 229.

p. 73. L.A. Reid (1895-) educated Aberdeen Grammar School, The Leys School, Cambridge and the University of Edinburgh where he won a wide number of prizes; he went on to teach philosophy at University College, Aberystwyth, Stanford Unversity, California, the University of Liverpool, the University of Newcastle and, from 1947-1962 at the University of London's Institute of Education; he retired in 1962. At the time Sir Richard was writing, Professor Reid was at the University of Newcastle where he taught from 1932-1947.

p. 74. Lippmann, *op cit.*

p. 76. Horace, *Epistles,* I. I, 65. Quintus Horatius Flaccus (65-68 B.C.) is remembered as a poet not only for his *Epistles* but for his *Odes, Epodes, Satires,* and *Ars Poetica.*

p. 77. *Expellas furca, tamen usque recurret* may be translated 'Thrust it out with a pitch-fork, and it will still come back without stopping.'

p. 78. Tacitus, *Agricola*, § 2. Titus Flavius Domitian (51-96) succeeded his brother, Titus, as Roman Emperor in 81. He became a tyrant and, assuming the titles 'dominus et deus' demanded public worship. During the last years of his reign a persecution of Christians erupted and tradition has it that it was during this period that the Apostle John, exiled at Patmos, received the revelations which he recorded in the Apocalypse.

Genesis, ch. 3, v. 5.

p. 80. Plato, *Phaedrus*, § 258. Jowett, *Dialogues*, II. 136.

p. 82. J.W. Adamson, *A Short History of Education* (Cambridge, 1930), pp. 30, 308.

Isaac Leon Kandel in *The Report of the Consultative Committee on Secondary Education*, p. 427. Professor Kandel (1881-1965) was educated at Manchester Grammar School, the University of Manchester and Columbia University, New York City. From 1923-1946 he was professor in the Teachers College of Columbia University. He was the author of several works on education.

Ghosts was the third of the 'problem plays' by the Norwegian playwright, Henrik Ibsen (1828-1906). Like his other famous plays it examined the 'problem' of people at odds with society.

p. 84. The resolution Livingstone had in mind was that proposed by John Dunning (1731-1783), M.P. for Calne, on 6 April 1780. The Resolution was that 'it is necessary to declare, that the influence of the crown has increased, is increasing, and ought to be diminished'. The Commons adopted it by a vote of 233 to 215, a majority of 18. Dunning, a Whig, was created Baron Ashburton two years later.

The Spens Report (pp 254 f) condemned it, but unfortunately failed to sentence it to death.

p. 86*. 'There is a considerable number of secondary schools in which the subject (religious instruction) is not included in the time-table of the higher Forms. In some of the latter religious instruction is discontinued in the Sixth Form only; in others it is discontinued in the year in which the School Certificate Examination is taken, or even earlier.' Report of the Consultative Committee on Secondary Education (1938), p. 207. [Since 1938 the situation has manifestly deteriorated far further than Sir Richard could have imagined when he included this footnote. Ed.].

p. 86†. John Dewey [J. Ratner ed], *Education Today* (London, 1941),

p. 52. John Dewey (1859-1952) was an American educator, philosopher, socialist writer and theoretician. He saw man as a biological entity and based his views on 'scientific realism'. There was little room for religion in his views on education, which he saw more as specialist training for the 'modern world' etc.

p. 88. Plato, *Laws*, § 643-4. Jowett, *Dialogues*, V. 213. Jowett translates 'excellence' as 'virtue' *(areté)*.

G.L.B.O.C. [George Berkeley], *Siris: A Chain of Philosophical Reflexions and Inquiries Concerning the Virtues of Tar Water*... (Dublin, 2nd edn, improved and corrected, 1744), §350, p. 143. The passage should read 'Whatever the world thinks, he who hath not much meditated upon God, the Humane mind, and the *Summum bonum,* may possibly make a thriving earthworm, but will most indubitably make a sorry patriot and a sorry statesman.' Berkeley (1685-1753), who was Bishop of Cloyne, was one of the leading philosophers of the 18th century. *Siris,* was first published in 1744. The term *Summum Bonum,* meaning in Latin the highest or greatest good, is used by philosophers to indicate, as here, the fundamental truths of man's existence.

p. 89. Thucydides, *History*, II. §39, 40. Livingstone's translation is based on that by Zimmern in The World Classics edn., pp. 112-3.

Prof. Sir John Adams, *Evolution of Educational Theory* (London 1912, in 'The Schools of Philosophy' series ed. by Sir Henry Jones); the only book by Sir Cyril Norwood in either the Bodleian Library Catalogue or the British Library Catalogue is *The English Tradition of Education* (London, 1929) and this is presumably the book to which Sir Richard was referring; Sir Thomas Percy Nunn, *Education: its Data and First Principles* (London, 1st edn. 1920, in 'The Modern Educator's Library' series; rev edn 1930).

p. 90. Thucydides, *History*, II. §40. Livingstone's translation is based on that by Zimmern in The World Classics edn., p. 113.

Edmund Burke, 'Thoughts on the Cause of the Present Discontents' in F.W. Raffety [ed], *The Works of the Right Honourable Edmund Burke* (Oxford, 1906, World Classics), II. 86. The pamphlet was written in 1770.

p. 92. The Association of Education Committees and the National Union of Teachers, *The Extra Year* (London, 1938), p. 114.

p. 93. Eric Gill, *Autobiography* (London, 1940), pp. 26, 28. the second passage quoted should read 'We are educated by the doing not by the learning. And that is, in my mind, the whole secret of education, whether in schools or in workshops or in life.' The sculptor, philosopher and writer, Eric Gill (1882-1940), was born the son of a nonconformist (Countess of Huntingdon) minister; he entered the priesthood of the Church of England and in 1913 left it for the Roman Catholic Church. He is still remembered for his Stations of the Cross in Westminster Cathedral.

p. 94. *There are valuable suggestions and discussions for the subject in* Education for Citizenship in Secondary Schools *(published under the auspics of the Association for Education in Citizenship); I do not agree with all its conclusions.*

p. 95. *The Extra Year,* p. 115.

p. 96*. *ibid.*, p. 120 f.

p. 96†. Aristotle, *Metaphysics*, §1072 b.

p. 97. Revelation, ch. 21, v. 2.

Thucydides, *History*, II. §43. Livingstone's translation is based on that by Zimmern in The Oxford World Classics edn., p. 115.

The word rendered 'powers' is the untranslatable ἀρεταί [aretaí], *a man's 'virtues', 'excellences' or 'gifts'. Cf. p. 66ff.*

p. 98. Plato [Cornford tr.], *The Republic*, pp. 159 ff: *slightly altered and shortened. Plato is speaking of the unity of feeling in his ruling class; but his words have a wider extension.*

p. 99. Burke. *Thoughts...Present Discontents*, p. 9.

p. 100. The text referred to is The Epistle to the Romans, ch. 12, v. 5: 'So we, being many, are one body in Christ, and every one members one of another.'

p. 102. Plato, *Laws*, §791-2. Jowett, *Dialogues,* V. 360-1.

p. 103. *The Times*, 29 Nov 1937.

For an informed criticism of the newer universities see Adolf Löwe, The Universities in Transformation *(London, 1941, no. 9 in the 'Christian News-Letter Books') — an important book — and D. M. Paton,* Blind Guides? A Student Looks at the University *(London, 1939).*

p. 104. *I doubt if this* [the attitude of superiority] *is true of English 'intellectuals'.*